# The
# African
# Grey
# Parrot
## Handbook

**Mattie Sue Athan and Dianalee Deter**

With Color Photography
Drawings by Michele Earle-Bridges

BARRON'S

**Dedication**
For my friend, Dan Gray. M.S.A.
For Marci, Huey, and Bob. Special thanks to Hanna, Sharon, and Toto. D.L.D.

*All inquiries should be addressed to:*
Barron's Educational Series, Inc.
250 Wireless Boulevard
Hauppauge, New York 11788
**http://www.barronseduc.com**

International Standard Book No. 0-7641-0993-6

*Library of Congress Catalog Card No. 99-48374*

**Library of Congress Cataloging-in-Publication Data**
Athan, Mattie Sue.
    The African grey parrot handbook / Mattie Sue Athan and Dianalee Deter ; with color photography ; drawings by Michele Earle-Bridges.
        p.  cm.
    Includes bibliographical references (p.      ).
    ISBN 0-7641-0993-6 (alk. paper)
    1. African grey parrot. I. Deter, Dianalee. II. Title.
SF473.P3 A8365    2000
636.6'865—dc21                                    99-48374
                                                        CIP

Printed in Hong Kong

9 8 7 6 5 4 3

## About the Authors

Mattie Sue Athan has studied behavior in companion parrots since 1978. Her area of special interest is the development of companion parrot behavior. Her book *Guide to a Well-Behaved Parrot,* published by Barron's Educational Series, Inc., has been called the "bible of pet bird behavior." She also wrote *Guide to Companion Parrot Behavior* and *Guide to the Quaker Parrot,* both published by Barron's Educational Series, Inc.

Dianalee Deter has a bachelor of science degree in zoology from the University of Florida. She began working with parrots in 1986, and owns "Paradise Found," a bird store in Westminster, Colorado. She is the co-author of *Guide to the Senegal Parrot and Its Family,* published by Barron's Educational Series, Inc.

## Photo Credits

Susan Green: pages 4, 10, 11, 18, 21, 24, 27, 30, 100, 120, 129, 139; Joan Balzarini: pages 5, 7, 19, 22, 25, 29, 32, 41, 42, 45, 58, 59, 69, 76, 127, 132, 158; Dianalee Deter: pages 9, 13, 20, 32, 35, 38, 47, 48, 50, 54, 56, 60, 65, 67, 71, 73, 74, 79, 82, 85, 105, 106, 109, 111, 119, 125, 136, 141, 143; Isabelle Francais: pages 6, 14, 17, 52, 92, 94, 97, 102, 114, 151.

## Cover Credits

Front cover: Joan Balzarini and Susan Green; Inside front cover: Joan Balzarini; Inside back cover: Joan Balzarini; Back cover: Joan Balzarini and Susan Green.

# Contents

# Preface

This book is a practical guide to living with African grey parrots with an emphasis on maintaining companion behavior. It is compiled from notes spanning over 30 years of combined experience with greys. Where scientific research has been available to document these observations, we have tried to cite that research. However, it is unlikely that many of the issues we are discussing here will ever be studied in a laboratory. We have relied, instead, on practical, hands-on experience with the birds.

Grey parrots are different. These intelligent birds can be more sensitive than most other common companion parrots. You may see techniques, observations, and strategies here that differ somewhat from those used in behavioral therapy for other types of parrots.

No space in this manuscript has been given over to demeaning the theories or techniques of others. Rather, we have used all available space to describe successful techniques and strategies from the collective experience of the authors. We know that much of what is written here must be considered "new territory," as we will be discussing and describing things in this text that may not have been previously discussed in print. Since we have often described concepts here that have not been commonly studied, we expect that this text will be frequently updated, adjusted, or corrected as new information becomes available.

# Chapter One

# The Grey Parrots: Out of Africa

## General Description

For centuries, grey parrots have enjoyed a reputation for extreme intelligence, ability to repeat words, and to use words with understanding. These sturdy birds reproduce readily in captivity and are usually available almost any place parrots are commonly kept. As companions they easily command a respected position in the human household.

There are two subspecies: the African grey (*Psittacus erithacus crithacus*), commonly called the Red-tailed grey, and the smaller Timneh African grey parrot (*Psittacus erithacus timneh*). The larger subspecies, (*Psittacus erithacus erithacus*), is sometimes erroneously called the "Congo" African grey in the United States. This bird has a distinct red tail and a solid black beak. The African grey parrot has a bare white face patch and sometimes bright, usually pale, silvery-yellow eyes. Both subspecies produce powder down for preening, not unlike the powder on cockatoo feathers. Many of the bird's gray contour feathers are edged with white, giving the bird a lacy or scalloped appearance. Especially in the red-tailed birds, there is significant color variation between individual birds, which may be light silver or almost black depending upon the point of origin of their ancestors.

Members of the larger subspecies, called here "the African grey" or the "Red-tailed grey," are said to be somewhat sexually dimorphic. However, ambiguous and crossover coloration occurs frequently, especially among birds with different ancestry, and DNA analysis rather than markings remains the best way to determine gender. Both subspecies possess equal talking abilities, with some individuals exhibiting exceptional mimicking and communication skills.

The tail of the Timneh African grey (*Psittacus erithacus timneh*) has a brownish wash over red, sometimes giving it a maroon appearance. The Timneh has a black-tipped, dark rosy-pink or horn-colored maxilla and a solid black mandible. The iris may be more silver than yellow. The Timneh is usually more active and

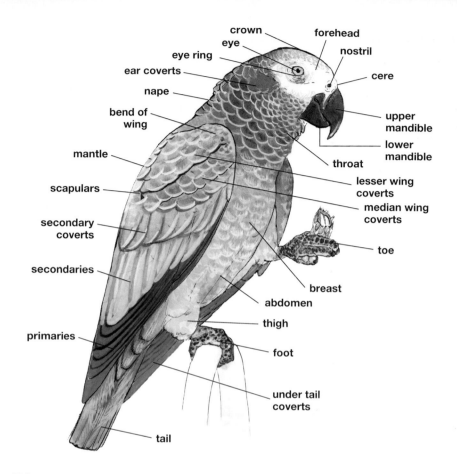

*African grey parrot anatomy.*

behaviorally stolid than the Red-tailed grey. Timnehs may learn to talk earlier than Red-tails and may be more inclined to talk in the presence of strangers. In our experience, Timnehs have less tendency to develop both ongoing fearfulness and feather-chewing disorders than the Red-tailed African greys.

While many are attracted by the grey parrot's reputation for intelligence, not everyone is immediately taken with the birds' appearance. The relatively small head, scalloped neck, and bare face patch have been called by some "vulturelike" or "snaky." The mature bird's silver or yellow eyes may look intimidating, but the big black eyes of a baby grey parrot can melt the heart of any discriminating parrot lover.

Possibly because of their extreme intelligence, grey parrots can develop a surprising diversity of

## Alex's Game

African greys are known to frequently possess and display a great love of tricks and games. The smarter the bird, the more potential it has to find ways to enjoy "tricking" humans. It would stand to reason, therefore, that Dr. Pepperberg's bird, Alex, probably knows a surprising number of tricks to play on humans. However, it hadn't occurred to me that a bird that lives in a university laboratory and that interacts daily with very intelligent, well-educated people would spend two days trying to trick me into breaking the rules.

As I awkwardly negotiated the disinfectant procedures, when visiting Alex, he could immediately recognize me as a newcomer, and "easy pickins" for mischief. Regarding me through first one oblong, slitty eye, then another, Alex bobbed his head and treated me to a loud, tonally correct wolf whistle. Both parts.

Then he stopped, looked again, and waited. I was just about to pucker up to respond with my own whistle when Dr. Pepperberg put her hand on my arm and shook her head "no."

Alex immediately repeated only the first half of the wolf whistle, regarding me with expectant mischief in his eyes. Again, Dr. Pepperberg shook her head "no."

You see, those who study Alex's language skills have decided not to engage in whistling with Alex in the laboratory because it might interfere with his desire to use human words which are more difficult to form. Newcomers are usually unaware of the rules, and Alex knows that they can sometimes be tricked into playing whistling games.

Again, and again during the few treasured hours I visited, Alex tried to "sucker" me into forbidden whistling interactions. It wasn't easy to ignore his charming, innovative, invitational whistles. It was extremely difficult to take Dr. Pepperberg's instruction, for Alex can be demanding in his quest for self-rewarding interactions. I guess he knows that all work and no play might make Alex a "dull boy." In fact, Dr. Pepperberg says that Alex is very dedicated in his quest for self-rewarding behaviors, spending many more hours playing than working.

both wanted and unwanted behaviors. In these birds, very creative, neurotic-seeming behaviors can appear almost spontaneously. The grey's reputation for intelligence might also be linked to the bird's reputation as the most "opinionated" bird, for even if a grey does not talk, it will still be exceptionally capable of communicating its preferences: African greys are often famous finicky eaters, manipulators, sticklers for routine, and gender chauvinists.

*Psittacus erithacus erithacus, the Red-tailed African grey, has a solid black beak, gray body, and distinctive red tail.*

Sound variations are produced when the bird changes the shape of the trachea. This requires practice. A baby grey rehearses quietly, babbling, muttering, or whispering, until it is confident enough to loudly produce the sounds it likes. While a particular baby parrot might learn a few words before it is weaned, most greys probably acquire their first words at about 11 months.

# Using Words with Understanding

Until the work of Dr. Irene Pepperberg, most parrot authorities were careful to use the word "mimic" rather than "talk" when referring to a parrot's abilities. It took a Harvard-educated Ph.D. to demonstrate to the scientific community what companion parrot owners knew all along: that African grey parrots can, indeed, use words with understanding.

For over 19 years, Dr. Pepperberg has studied and statistically analyzed the African grey parrot's speaking abilities. Working first with Alex, a "second-hand" grey from a pet store, Dr. Pepperberg evaluated the bird's abilities to answer questions about familiar objects, their shape, number, substance, and color. But Dr. Pepperberg didn't only evaluate talking; she also documented methods by which birds acquire human speech. Especially, she has observed that grey parrots

Like other intelligent species—humans, chimpanzees, elephants, whales—the baby grey's intellectual and behavioral development requires a relatively long time. Likewise, talking skills in greys develop a little more slowly than some other parrots. Juvenile greys are not considered emotionally and behaviorally independent until approximately two years.

Parrots have no vocal cords. Sounds are produced when air is forced across the top of the trachea, a process that resembles blowing across the top of a soda bottle.

learn best when competing against a rival. This explains another generally accepted phenomenon: Although a grey parrot can and will sometimes speak in the voice of a favorite person, African greys commonly acquire more words in the voice of a rival. Dr. Pepperberg's most famous work with the model/rival method uses competition to stimulate language acquisition and use in the African grey parrot.

The African grey must be protected from learning unpleasant human sounds such as squeals, squeaks, screeches, burps, belches, and worse. The bird must also be protected from learning profanity, for it will probably outlive humans in the household and will say in its next home what it heard in the first. Greys must also be protected from learning screaming from other parrots and barking from dogs, as they repeat these kinds of noises frequently and with great relish.

# Behavior

### Behavioral Training

Companion greys must learn cooperation, acceptance of change, and independent play in order to fully enjoy life in the living room. This behavioral training occurs with consistent handling, redundant patterning, and sensitive environmental manipulations as described in this book and in *Guide to a Well-Behaved Parrot*, and *Guide to Com-panion Parrot Behavior*, both by the co-author of this book, Mattie Sue Athan (see Useful Addresses and Literature, page 165). While tendencies toward aggression are expected and usually considered somewhat "normal," developing fearfulness must be treated immediately, for this can lead to unwelcome stress reactions.

Expect to treat a baby grey almost exactly as you would treat a child in the home. Never punish the bird, especially by hitting, squirting, or dropping. Even "the evil eye" (see

*An adult Timneh grey has a rose or horn colored maxilla and is usually darker than the Red-tailed subspecies.*

page 121) and "time-outs" (see page 121) can be frightening for an extremely sensitive grey. An African grey is an undomesticated animal, and it may respond to perceived violence as though it feared for its life.

The bird must be patterned to appropriate behaviors by example and reward, practice and repetition. Fortunately, this is usually easily accomplished in a properly weaned, normally experimental, well-socialized hand-fed juvenile grey. During the first three to six months in the home, a hand-fed grey should be curious and eager to please. This is the juvenile developmental period sometimes called "the honeymoon period," the period during which confidence gradually turns from approval seeking to independence and the instinct to dominate. This period is an especially good time to avoid anything resembling punishment, for, as with a human child, the African grey has memory and is perfectly capable of holding a grudge.

# Parrots in the Wild

Habitat loss and humans are primary causes for the decline of grey parrots in the wild. Comparing charts of the bird's range between 1976 (de Graul) and 1998 (Juniper and Parr) the birds appear to have lost habitat on the northern and southern reaches of the range and expanded with agriculture to the east.

Although grey parrots were the second most heavily traded parrot in the world in the 1980s, they are still common where large tracts of forest remain and are still numerous in some areas, especially in the Congo basin rain forests. Habitat loss in some parts of their range, such as from Nigeria to Sierra Leone, and extensive trapping have lead to population declines, especially around towns and cities.[1]

Grey parrots commonly inhabit lowland forests, although they often

*Juvenile Red-tailed greys have dark eyes and black tips on the tail feathers. Red spots on the thighs are often temporary.*

visit open land adjacent to woodlands. They go to the ground with caution, circling a clearing, sometimes twice before landing. They are known to pick up quartz from the ground[2] and go to the ground to drink at elephant wallows and pathways.[3] Wild grey parrots are extremely shy and rarely allow humans to approach.

The wild grey's native diet includes mostly high-occurring fruits such as oil-palm (*Elaeis guinensis*) nuts, other nuts, seeds, fruits, and berries. They are famous for damaging maize crops. When they can be seen, grey parrots are often observed carrying oil-palm nuts and other prized foods long distances before consuming them.

The birds often roost in large groups, often calling loudly during mornings and evenings and in flight.

Flocks are described as very noisy. Greys frequently roost in trees over water, even being said to prefer roosting on islands in rivers. Flocking behavior is most often reported outside breeding season.

Most nesting is probably solitary, although greys have been seen nesting in large groups with only one pair per tree. De Graul reports that offspring are usually produced during or just after the rainy season.[4] Juniper and Parr suggest that breeding season varies with locale and that dry season breeding is common in some areas.[5] De Graul also reports that "...nesting trees inherited by those born in them once existed and perhaps still do in certain areas, as is the case in South America with the macaws."

De Graul reports that grey parrots are also sometimes harassed, or

*Offer young greys enticing toys and praise them for displaying curiosity.*

perhaps preyed upon, by the Palm-nut Vulture (*Gypohierax angolensis*), also called sometimes the "Vulture Eagle." This bird was once classified with vultures, but later has been called an eagle. Since the Palmnut Vulture is not nimble enough to catch a grey easily, reported scenes of grey parrots fleeing the larger birds in panic may be related to territorial disputes rather than predation.

In the past, natives sold grey parrots and often even hand-fed and trained them. However, they did not keep them as pets. Legal importation of grey parrots into the United States ended in 1992. Greys are still legally trapped and exported from some parts of Africa to countries other than the United States.

# Grey Parrots as Companions

Somewhere between the jungle and the living room is the Brave New World of the companion grey—a creature that lives in human homes, developing both communication and cooperation skills while pursuing its very own agenda. The behaviors with which the regal grey pursues that personal agenda are genetically programmed and make the addition of a grey parrot more like adding a child or a spouse than adding a pet.

A companion grey is not a pet. It's an exotic, undomesticated animal that exhibits instinctual wild characteristics, especially instinctual behaviors related to reproduction that do not usually appear in pet dogs and cats. Although young parrots often exhibit behaviors that seem to be motivated by a desire to please, these behaviors are actually motivated by a desire to belong to a flock, as this means safety. As the bird matures, its behaviors will become increasingly selfish.

As with dogs and horses, early and enduring behavior training can minimize the development of unwelcome instinctual behaviors as the birds mature. Without ongoing behavioral support, many, possibly most, companion grey parrots will gradually or quickly revert to instinctual wild behaviors or will adapt some unfortunate behaviors to replace wild behaviors. Some wild behaviors fit in well in the living room environment; some do not. Since grey parrots live such a long time, up to 50 years, the acquisition of only one difficult-to-live-with behavior every year or two can produce an obnoxious bird by the time it's a teenager.

Today's companion greys are at most, two generations out of the wild. The behaviors they improvise are generated by instincts that enabled their ancestors to survive in the wild. The wild parrot lived, loved, learned, and evolved through thousands of generations in order to have the skills necessary to meet nature's challenges. Wild parrots must learn a diverse assortment of transportation and communication skills; they must know how to find

*An African grey expects to be included in "flock" activities such as mealtime.*

and separate good food from toxic plants; they must know how to defend territory, how to recognize and avoid predators, how to find safe water, and how to rejoin their families when separated. They must be able to do all this sometimes in blinding rain or oppressive drought. They must face the challenges of finding and keeping a mate alive, of developing role-appropriate behaviors, of competing for and defending nesting sites, and of creating, nurturing, and teaching their extremely helpless offspring to do the same. They must have some mechanism by which to evaluate the food supply in order to determine whether a nesting process should be completed.

A very different set of behaviors are necessary for survival in the living room.

## Learning Indoor Survival Skills

There's a very real temptation to believe that because a weaned juvenile grey parrot is "perfect" when it comes home, it will stay that way. The dependent baby will mature into a creature that strives to be a productive member of the flock. Left undirected, these activities include chewing nest sites and foraging areas, such as furniture or computer parts, calling the "flock"—screaming when the owner leaves the room—joining in vocal social interactions—outtalking the telephone or TV—and allopreening—removing moles or jewelry. Without planning or behavior training, grey parrots can easily develop a wide range of behaviors that don't contribute either to a happy life or to good behavioral adjustment.

## Weaning

A premium hand-fed baby grey should be weaned completely before going to its new home (see Coming Home, page 21). While there is no magical age at which this happens, it usually occurs some time between four and seven months of age. Some birds may take more time, but rarely less time, to be physically and emotionally weaned. Birds that have been allowed to fully fledge (fly) will usually develop the confidence necessary to successfully change homes earlier.

There is a window of opportunity of about eight to ten weeks after weaning during which the bird will willingly change role models (flock/home). Most breeder/dealers prefer to sell greys during this window. A grey parrot over nine months old may be reluctant to change a parent-baby bond and too young to abandon that bond for a mate-type bond. These birds can usually go easily and successfully to new homes during or after they have completed their first wing feather molt at 12 to 18 months.

## Appropriate Age to Begin Training

Behavioral training should be started even before the bird goes to its new home, and continued in the same way within the first few days of arriving in the new home. There's a window of opportunity for teaching a young grey both human-interactive behaviors and independence. In the wild, the young bird would be learning important skills during this period. Its brain is ready to be quickly filled with all the information it needs to survive. This is probably the most important developmental

*These juvenile Timneh greys act as a "support group," building confidence while encouraging each other to explore in an atmosphere of security.*

period in the bird's life, for if appropriate skills are not learned at this time, the wild bird will not survive.

If behavioral training is neglected during these early days, then either aggression, shyness, overbonding, excessive vocalizations, or other acquired misbehaviors can develop. If the new owner of a grey parrot has not planned the bird's environment and begun behavioral training within the bird's first six months in the home, it will begin improvising behaviors that may or may not contribute to its full and happy participation as a human companion. Inappropriate behaviors must be addressed either before they appear or immediately after.

# Step-up Practice

A successful companion grey parrot must learn both cooperation and independence. A hand-fed bird first learns cooperation by being fed by humans. The weaned juvenile should be able to expect that food and water will always be available. How, then, are cooperation skills generated and reinforced after weaning?

From its first days in the home, the baby grey should enjoy practicing the step-up routine for at least a minute or two most days. The bird's enjoyment of the process is a very necessary part of this interaction.

Unless a bird is cooperative enough and well patterned enough to step up from an unfamiliar perch in unfamiliar territory, it may refuse to

*Step-up practice encourages trust, cooperation, and respect.*

step up from the cage or other familiar perch. Step-up practice may initially have to take place outside the bird's established territory. A laundry room or hallway is usually perfect, as the bird will probably never spend much time in these types of areas, and therefore should not develop territorial behavior in them. A cooperative bird can be successfully patterned to this exercise anywhere it feels safe. Good behavioral strategies for the future include practice stepping up the bird:

**1.** From the hand to and from an unfamiliar perch

**2.** From hand to hand

**3.** From a hand-held perch to and from an unfamiliar perch

**4.** From a hand-held perch to a hand-held perch

**5.** From a familiar perch to and from both hands and to and from hand-held perches.

Be sure to offer affection and praise after each completed step-up. Always discontinue step-up practice only after a successful completion of the command. This is crucial to good patterning. If the command is not successful, technique, approach, or prompting mannerisms must be altered. Do not continue with unsuccessful methods. Be careful not to reinforce unsuccessful patterns.

There is no substitute for warm, genuine human enthusiasm as a reward for the bird's success in stepping up; like other effective behavioral strategies, step-ups must be practiced consistently and sensitively. Step-up practice inspires, facilitates, and habituates cooperation in a baby parrot. The predictability of human and bird responses to one another provides a comfortable standard for all other interactions. Each human expecting to interact with the bird should practice step-ups most days for a minute or so and in a routine variety of ways. Especially with shy or cautious birds, as many grey parrots are, the bird's enjoyment of the process is absolutely necessary. If the bird is not eagerly, or at least willingly, cooperating with step-ups and step-up practice, something is wrong, and you should seek professional help.

An effective relationship with a grey must begin with and maintain both mutual trust and respect. If bird and humans achieve no mutual respect, the relationship is lost. If, for example, the baby parrot begins to treat a human like a piece of property rather than a respected flock-

mate, everybody could be in trouble. Although most grey parrots go through a nippy stage—this is part of the normal development of independence and personality in many juvenile hookbills—the appearance of biting behaviors around a particular person or location can signal the development of territorial or bonding-related aggression.

Frequent, exciting, and/or soothing verbal reinforcement are necessary components of successful step-up practice. Reinforcing the bird to enjoy step-up practice not only acts to prevent the development of aggression, but also prevents the occasional development of shyness. While an aggressive juvenile parrot gains cooperation skills from step-ups, the shy or fearful bird can learn confidence from the joy and predictability of the interaction.

## Toweling

Early patterning is also necessary to prevent the development of stress reactions to toweling (see Towel Technique on page 30). A companion parrot requires annual veterinary examinations and grooming at least twice yearly. Cuddling, snuggling, and playing "Peek-a-bird" in a towel will improve trust and condition the baby to be more tolerant of being restrained during these potentially stressful interactions.

We must be empathetic and predictable in the handling of all baby parrots, but the maintenance of trust is especially important to the greys. These birds sometimes tend to exhibit extreme responses. Red-tails, and, to a lesser extent, Timnehs, have an occasional tendency to suddenly acquire surprising fearful behaviors (see section on Fearfulness, page 55). Use extra care and consistency with grey parrots to compensate for this sensitivity.

# Bonding and Socialization

In order to maintain an interactive disposition, it's important to avoid allowing a grey parrot to become overly possessive of a particular human or territory. The bird should have relationships with many humans and other safe animals, and should spend as much time as possible in diverse locations inside and out of the home. Early socialization to enjoy changes in the cage and home environment, access to appropriate choices, and bird-safe outings to meet sensitive, interactive humans will acclimate the bird to tolerate the inevitable twists of fate that plague all creatures.

Interacting vocally is an important part of bonding with the flock. Vocal behaviors—babbling or talking—can develop almost any time before or after weaning. The vocalization might include some annoying whistles, but will probably not include screaming. While these interactive behaviors stimulate talking, they can turn into irritating, attention-demanding noises. Independent play must be encour-

aged by providing interesting tools (toys).

Appropriate human behavior also stimulates appropriate behavior in companion greys. If humans in the household demonstrate play and communication skills in constructive ways, the grey parrot will likely learn to do the same. In other words, if humans use screaming, domination, and force in their interactions with the bird, it will likely learn to do the same. It might also develop fearful responses.

## Chewing and Messiness

Grey parrots are cavity breeders; they lay eggs and raise babies in hollowed out, mostly wooden, spaces. When a cavity-breeding parrot is gleefully turning the price-less antique clock into toothpicks, it's really saying, "Look how sexy I

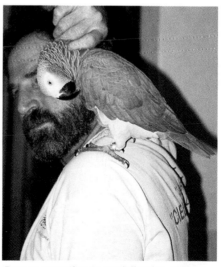

*Proper attention to socialization and meeting the parrot's needs can result in a grey that is a cherished family member.*

am! I would be a fantastic mate. I could make a nice big nest cavity for you and our babies."

Providing a grey with appropriate chewables will help save the furniture and woodwork. Providing for chewing behaviors will help to prevent biting, excessive vocalization, nail biting, overpreening, feather chewing, and other innovated displacement behaviors.

Chewing and its ugly cousin, messiness, are innate behaviors, not behavior problems. They must be accepted and accommodated because they are part of the parrot's nature that cannot be changed. A good-quality cage is especially important here. The cage may be the most significant factor in whether or not the bird succeeds in its first home. A hard-to-clean cage can easily inspire resentment in humans responsible for cleaning and can damage the human/bird bond. (For more on cages, see page 63.)

# Would You Enjoy a Grey Parrot's Companionship?

A grey parrot is a wild (undomesticated) animal and not necessarily a perfect companion for every human. The bird must be trained to cooperate, guided to emotional independence, and accommodated for its natural behaviors. If you love planning, playing chess, and other forms of strategy, you would probably love a grey. If you think you could tolerate an occasional temper tantrum and are willing to put up with some damaged possessions and mess in order to share the company of sublime feathered joy, then a grey parrot might be perfect for you.

The potential behavior problems discussed here are usually very easily prevented. A new grey parrot owner who applies the principles set forth in this book might never see a habitual problem behavior.

*Fuzzy babies with big black eyes can be irresistible.*

[1] Tony Juniper and Mike Parr, *Parrots, a Guide to Parrots of the World*. Yale University Press, New Haven and London, 1998, p. 376.

[2] Joseph M. Forshaw, *Parrots of the World*. T.F.H. Publications, 1978, pp. 287–288.

[3] *Parrot's: Look Who's Talking*. Thirteen/ WNET and BBC-TV, Video, 1995.

[4] Wolfgang de Graul, *The Grey Parrot*. T.F.H. Publications, 1987.

[5] Tony Juniper, and Mike Parr. *Parrots, a Guide to Parrots of the World*. Yale University Press, New Haven and London, 1998, pp. 375–376.

## Chapter Two

# Selecting and Socializing a Grey Parrot

Fluff-covered baby greys like to stretch their long necks to see over the sides of their containers. Their big black eyes and soft whimpers are an unmistakable invitation to pick them up and cuddle them. When someone does come along and snuggles them, they make it more than obvious how appreciated the attention is. Neonatal (unweaned) baby greys have a way of melting human hearts; therefore, it is best not to pick up a baby grey while holding a credit card until a few other details have been determined.

## Selecting the Source

A grey parrot can be an expensive, occasionally intrusive, and long-lived acquisition. Don't rush into a decision. It's usually best to decide *where* to get the bird before selecting one. The start a baby grey receives influences its ability to cope with life as a companion to humans.

Carefully examine the establishment the bird is coming from so that you are confident that the needs of the bird, as well as your needs, are being met.

• Before going home, the baby must be fully weaned onto a healthy diet (see page 80).

• The bird should be well acclimated to its own cage and responding curiously to toys.

• A juvenile grey will have a better sense of confidence if its wings and nails have not been groomed too short.

• Expect a written health guarantee of at least a week after taking the baby home.

A conscientious bird seller can be reasonably expected to provide easy access to information about care and training.

### Dealers

Dealers who care most about the quality of homes their babies go into are likely to have done a thorough and effective job all around, including crucial early socialization and weaning. Many aviaries require an appointment to see birds. Some dealers require applications from potential owners and strict requirements that new owners have to meet. Some breeders now require that new parrot owners attend classes before being allowed to take a bird home.

**1.** Observe shopper's etiquette. If possible, bathe and change clothes and shoes between each store or aviary you visit.

**2.** Politely observe house rules for handling baby birds, which may include asking first to handle a baby, washing or disinfecting your hands, and stepping through disinfectant to minimize possible disease transmission.

**3.** Don't provoke the birds by waving fingers in their faces.

When selecting neonates, follow the breeder's handling instructions precisely, as the babies are best handled in familiar ways: After carefully washing your hands, talk softly and move carefully; play eye games (see page 120). Once they are moving around well, baby greys should start responding by turning toward the person talking and by answering back. Sometimes the babies will come running over, but this depends on how many strangers they've seen recently. Avoid babies that stay cowered in the corner, fearing interaction.

Newly weaned juveniles still have black eyes that later fade to gray and finally turn variable shades of yellow by the time the bird is two years old. While some individuals' eyes change quickly and some do not, if the eyes are not yet yellow, the bird is still very young. Baby Red-tails have black on the edges of their tail feathers. Baby Timnehs' tail feathers are often almost completely black.

When considering and evaluating a fully weaned grey parrot, be respectful because of your stranger status. It's not unusual for a content juvenile grey to not want to come off a familiar perch or out of a familiar cage to be with a stranger. It's better if someone known to the bird picks it up and hands it to the newcomer.

# Initial Interactions

Initial interactions should be vocal and passive. Avoid putting fingers where the parrot might be tempted to bite them. The bird should look comfortable on a stranger's hand, but it is sometimes too much to ask to pet a grey parrot right away. If the bird has been properly raised and cared for, it is happy and secure where it is and has no reason to look for someone else to take care of it. This is not an indication that the bird will not bond. On the contrary, it's an indication that the parrot has a good sense of security and will be better adjusted when it does bond, although a baby grey might spend some time scratching curiously in corners. Avoid birds that jump to the floor or the bottom of the cage growling when approached.

# Evaluating the Chick

In addition to evaluating whether the bird has a good emotional and behavioral start, a prospective owner should perform a careful physical examination before deciding whether or not to buy a particular baby.

• Fluffy neonates should be plump and round. Fledging greys may seem a little thin, but not skinny. You should be able to feel, but not see the breastbone. Muscles on each side of the breastbone should feel firm and well fleshed.

• Eyes should be clear and black, round and watchful. The eyes will begin to change color after about four months. Some individuals may have silver eyes by the time they are seven or eight months old; others may have gray eyes for over eighteen months. This may be gender-related, with males' eyes changing faster.

• Nares (nostrils) should be clear of discharge. Breathing should be easy and uniform with no audible click.

• Beak should be straight and smooth. There should be no noticeable ridges on the exterior surface. Both Red-tails and Timnehs will have black beaks as neonates.

• Feathers may have some baby food stuck to them, as the powder down that helps them keep feathers clean has not yet come in.

• Juvenile coloring such as black on tails or red spots on thighs or breast may be apparent.

• Feet should have two toes pointing forward and two toes pointing back. They should have straight toes with sharp nails and no swollen joints or sores on the bottoms of the feet. Feet should open and close.

• There should be no feces caked around the vent.

• Droppings may have a lot of water associated with them since hand-feeding formulas are high in moisture, but all three parts, feces, urates, and urine, should be present and well formed.

• Don't be concerned about occasional stress bars across the long feathers of the wing or tail, but be

*Young greys have dark eyes and dark tips on the tail.*

*Bright eyed, healthy babies are alert and plump.*

wary of a bird with multiple stress bars on each feather, which might be an indication that the bird has been ill.

• Feathers should be uniformly shaped. The sheath of unopened developing feathers should be pointed and not rounded on the tips before the feather opens. Undeveloped feathers should be well attached and not easily bumped out by normal petting, as this could be a sign of illness. Mature birds should have powder on the feathers.

• The breeder should tell you if the youngster has been treated by a veterinarian for illness. This does not indicate that the bird is "sickly." Baby birds and elderly birds are the most susceptible to illness. There should be a health guarantee so that you can be assured by any veterinarian that the baby is healthy at the time it is taken to its new home.

# Food and Related Issues

African greys enjoy food in a much more intense way than most other domestic parrots. In a flock of mixed species, hand-fed parrots, the grey is the one with its face most often hidden in the food dish. Some juvenile greys spend so much time in the food dish that passersby might be prompted to ask if there is something wrong with the bird. Every piece of food will be chewed and sucked dry so that it looks like it went through a food processor and then dehydrated.

Allowing this interaction with food is important in the bird's development. An appropriate hand-feeding method allows the bird to experience food going into its mouth and down its throat. Tube- or gavage-feeding directly into the crop should be avoided unless necessary. Early exposure to the tastes and textures of food provides the young parrot with important information and stimulation. Solid food should be available to the baby well before weaning. Anyone purchasing a properly weaned juvenile grey should expect the bird to have had experience with a variety of healthy food items. The new owner should not have to put the new bird through the stresses of a diet change when bringing it home. The new parrot is best off if it is required to tolerate as few major changes as possible—and that includes its diet. (For more on diet, see page 80.)

**Note:** Grey parrots should not be taken home before they are weaned. While with other types of parrots the ability to eat solid food on their own is associated with independence, this is not usually true for greys. Once a baby grey has flown and is eating on its own, it then begins, under the supervision of its trusted "parent," to learn survival skills. In the living room this means playing with toys and vocalizing and other interactive behaviors. A baby grey, taken from its "parent" at this age is extremely vulnerable emotionally. To promote emotional stability in a grey, it should stay with its attentive human hand-feeder until at least 16 weeks of age. For many greys, the time should be much longer, for the bird is considered juvenile until it is 18 to 24 months old.

*A weaning grey needs a variety of nutritious food to play with, chew on, and, occasionally, eat.*

# Weaning, Confidence, and Constructive Interactions

African grey parrots, especially Red-tailed greys, are notorious for developing problematic behaviors such as feather chewing, fear reactions, shrieking, and repetitive/compulsive behaviors. Compassionate humans work hard to prevent these unsavory developments by providing for all their birds' needs in a timely manner. A suitable, well-positioned cage, easily gripped perches, a variety of toys, a diverse, nutritious diet, regular attention, appropriate grooming, and opportunities for exercise can fill the needs of most companion birds.

However, many greys that appear to have an ideal life with every possible need provided still develop neurotic behaviors, especially shredding, clipping, or pulling feathers. Many of these neurotic behaviors can be traced to failure to develop confidence during the weaning process.

## Companionship for the Baby Grey

A neonatal African grey is an intensely needy bird. An Amazon of comparable age might call when it's hungry and then go back to sleep once it's fed. However, a hand-feeding baby grey parrot might call for attention even though it is not yet hungry. A baby grey needs the reassurance of touch, to have its head rubbed, and to be snuggled. Greys often do much better if they are not raised alone and have another bird to snuggle with and to preen. A fuzzy neonatal grey with its down still mostly showing needs plenty of

*A baby grey will sometimes cry for snuggling even when its other needs have been met.*

comforting and snuggling. Many breeders and hand-feeders give an "only chick" grey parrot a safe stuffed animal to provide the physical and emotional support usually provided by a clutchmate.

Once the bird is covered with feathers, snuggling should give way to playing and learning. This is the perfect time to begin combining snuggling and playing peek-a-boo in a towel (see Towel Technique on page 30). This snuggling exercise, called the towel game, will be used later to provide an immediate sense of safety anytime it's needed.

## Attention

As the baby bird matures, it more readily shows curiosity and playfulness if it has a strong connection with its parent/hand-feeder and receives regular attention. Many people are worried that giving a young bird too much attention results in a "spoiled" bird that constantly demands attention. In most cases, however, it is not possible to give a baby grey too much attention, as long as much of that attention is constructive interaction such as playing games, engaging in enjoyable patterning routines, or modeling appropriate behaviors.

As the baby parrot becomes more mobile, it will be driven to copy the actions of an adult or of a perceived parent. The young bird requires a role model to follow and it derives security from being able to fill this need. The person playing the parent bird role must spend a lot of time actively involved in the bird's quest for knowledge. The baby grey will instinctively trust the acting "parent" to teach it and will be more open to the person who accepts that role.

The more time you spend helping the bird to develop a sense of curiosity, the more likely that the bird will be interested in new situations rather than being afraid of them. The more foods that are introduced to the youngster by its role model, the greater variety of foods the bird will willingly try later. The hand-feeder must teach the bird about food and toys and should allow the juvenile bird to develop observable confidence before sending it off to join a new "flock."

### Bonding with Your Parrot

In the past, it was sometimes presumed that for each owner, personally hand-feeding his or her own bird, was the best way to develop a strong bond with a companion parrot. This advice has led to many disappointments. Removing a baby from its parent during the most precarious learning situation undermines confidence. Additionally, many baby birds that were so carefully hand-fed, with all the worry and angst involved, switched bonds later. Any parrot will avoid forming a mate bond with its parent. The bird forms a parent/offspring bond with the hand-feeder/parent and mate/flock member bonds in the new home.

We can't say this often enough: the consequences of successfully weaning a grey parrot are so dire

*A soft toy can help an "only" chick feel more secure.*

that weaning should be left only to experienced professionals with all the resources necessary to produce a confident, interactive companion parrot.

# Coming Home

**Wing feathers:** Before bringing the weaned juvenile parrot home, ask the breeder or dealer to see that the bird's wing feathers are properly trimmed. For a grey, this means leaving enough feathers to allow safe gliding. Outside, a breeze can turn gliding into flying. A newly purchased juvenile grey does not belong outdoors unless it's in a cage or carrier.

**Temperature:** Find out what temperature the bird is accustomed to. If the weather is cold, warm up the car before taking the baby outside.

*A carefully weaned baby grey is ready to bond with its new family.*

Carry the bird in a rigid carrier that can be covered on the outside and can be belted into the car for safety. A mature companion grey can happily tolerate much cooler temperatures than most humans, but this is a baby grey enduring the stress of changing homes. For the first week or so, it's a good idea to keep the newly acquired juvenile a little warmer (about five degrees) than the usual anticipated room temperature.

**Quarantine:** Carefully quarantine the new bird to make sure it has no contact with any other birds in the home until the veterinarian says such interaction is not dangerous. Most veterinarians will probably recommend a quarantine period of at least 30 days.

**Veterinarians:** A responsible dealer will give a reasonable guarantee of the bird's health, but you should take the bird as soon as possible to an experienced avian veterinarian for a complete blood workup and any tests the veterinarian recommends. If the bird is not at least 16 weeks old, its immune system is not fully developed, and extra precautions must be taken. Try to schedule the veterinarian's first appointment in the morning so that the baby won't be exposed to dust from other birds. If possible, take the baby in its own cage and cover the outside bottom of the cage or carrier with a plastic garbage bag so that it won't leave or pick up germs when it is set down in the veterinarian's facility.

The veterinarian might suggest DNA testing to determine gender. Expect the veterinarian to recommend laboratory tests to verify the bird's health, including a test for PBFD (Psittacine Beak and Feather Disease, see page 96). The costs of diagnostic tests are not usually part of the bird's health guarantee from the seller, but they could save much expense and heartache later if the baby bird turns out to be harboring an unseen illness or disease. If diagnostic tests determine that the bird has a health problem, a responsible dealer honoring a guarantee will provide treatment. Some dealers will expect the bird to be returned for treatment or to be treated by the veterinarian they choose.

**Bands:** A loose-fitting band can be dangerous. Ask the veterinarian whether or not the bird's band fits properly or whether it should be removed. A bird without a band can have its DNA registered for identification purposes. Some veterinarians might suggest microchipping. We favor DNA registry for grey parrots because of occasional apparent adverse reactions to microchipping.

## Avoiding Moving Stress

Avoid as much stress as possible when relocating the parrot. Changing too many of the things that are important to the parrot can undermine the sense of security of even the most confident grey parrot. Ideally, the bird should go to its new home in a familiar cage with familiar toys to be fed familiar food by familiar people.

Provide an appropriate cage while waiting for the neonate to wean (see The Bird Cage on page 63). This way the baby can grow up in the cage it will occupy as a juvenile and will feel more secure in any surroundings. If the bird is already weaned and ready to go, the new caregiver should try to provide a cage as similar as possible to the one the bird has been living in. Or, the bird might be introduced to a new cage at least a week or two before leaving the place it knows. Again, beloved and familiar toys should be moved with the bird.

## Environmental Adjustments

During these early weeks and months, the juvenile grey develops its view of the environment. A bird that sees its environment as scary and unpredictable can quickly

*Leg bands are the most common form of traceable identification.*

develop a fear response to anything that seems unfamiliar. While these fear responses might serve the grey parrot well in the wild, where predators are waiting at every turn, those same fear responses are problematic in companion parrots. A young grey that has been carefully protected and nurtured through this time will be a more stable bird that will more easily weather the changes that occur naturally in life.

There should be a gradual transition between the perceived constant attention from the hand-feeder to the more limited attention available in the new home. If the bird is accustomed to spending the day out, it should begin spending a little more time in its cage while it is still with the hand-feeder.

When you take the youngster home, the juvenile grey's sense of security may be shaken. You must therefore take extra time helping the bird to feel comfortable in the new home. Each bird's adjustment time will vary. The young bird should not be left to fend for itself, physically or emotionally, right away. The human flock can reduce the amount of attention being provided as the bird becomes more comfortable.

**1.** Try to bring the juvenile grey home as early as possible during the day so that the bird can become accustomed to its surroundings before dark.

**2.** Keep a towel over about half of the cage for the first few days.

**3.** Provide the bird with a small night-light, especially if there are pets in the home that might move around in the dark. A bird that is disturbed at night and not getting

*The baby's new family can help him adjust to his new surroundings with comfort and reassurance.*

enough sleep will be physically and emotionally stressed. Consider the possibility of a separate place to sleep (see Roost Cage, page 68).

### Food

Warm foods such as oatmeal, cooked squash, or sweet potatoes can be very comforting to a newly weaned juvenile grey. In addition to offering the same diet it was on before coming into your home, offering warm "comfort foods" daily for a while will help provide a smooth transition to the new home, and most African greys will enjoy warm treats occasionally throughout their lives.

# Learning Independent and Social Behaviors

Most of the strategies that African greys use to get along in life are learned. Communicating, eating, learning how to play with toys and what to be afraid of all contribute to the development of independence. Many other types of birds are independent by nature; companion greys must learn independence through the compassionate encouragement of the social unit (caregivers).

When a young grey meets a new situation, it looks for cues as to how it should feel about that situation. If trusted humans are happy or excited, a grey will then usually not be afraid. The best way to instill the curiosity and confidence that are

*Baby greys encourage each other to explore and play. The new human family will take over this role.*

necessary for independence is for you as the caregiver to model them. You should also provide the young bird a safe haven from which to observe its surroundings when its confidence is shaky.

## Reassurance

When a new owner brings a weaned juvenile grey home, that bird needs plenty of reassurance. It needs to know that it can get the attention of its owners when it needs to and that it is a welcome member of this new flock. It is not unusual for a juvenile grey to revert to making baby noises to announce its needs.

A new bird owner might be afraid of "spoiling" the baby by responding to the cries, but, much like any other kind of baby, juvenile greys cry when they need something, and ignoring a crying baby can foster feelings of insecurity. The crying normally stops once the young bird feels secure.

## Promoting Curiosity and Independence

As the baby's confidence grows, so will its curiosity. It will depend on those around it to encourage it to develop an inquisitive nature. Unlike other parrots that will turn everything within reach into a toy, greys have to

## Beau and Elmo

A young couple came in one Saturday afternoon looking for a baby grey. Snuggling a five-week old Timneh on the young wife's lap, it was obviously love at first sight.

Sharon and her husband placed a deposit to hold Beau until he weaned. They came in regularly to visit and were well prepared when the day finally came to take him home.

About a month later she came in to say she was having problems with Beau. I was surprised and asked her what kind of problems. She blushed and stammered and looked sheepish.

While she was waiting for Beau to be ready to go home with her, she had fallen in love with a baby Red-tail that was still hand-feeding. That dealer let her take the bird, Elmo, home unweaned. When Beau saw the other baby hand-feeding, he wanted to be hand-fed as well. Now she had two hand-feeding baby greys and didn't know what to do to get them weaned.

With time and patience Elmo was weaned and Beau was weaned again. Elmo learned a lot from Beau, who has more than his share of self-confidence, and has not suffered much from the experience, but not all babies sold unweaned are as lucky as Elmo.

be taught to be this adventurous. You can model for the bird by playing with the toys and shredding them in front of the bird, at the same time, show excitement and delight vocally. While playing with the toy, the caregiver can periodically present the toy to the bird briefly, then take the toy back and play some more. This type of modeling is even more effective if there's another parrot, person, or pet to join in. When the second party begins playing with the toy, you can gush praises. The baby bird will then want to join in the flock's games. This same game can be played with new foods or any other new accessory.

Vocal games can also help promote independence. While the baby is quietly practicing by itself, pick up some of the pleasant sounds and repeat them back. The baby will stop to listen, but at the same time it will be encouraged to experiment more with this means of getting attention. Again, these interactive games encourage self-confidence, which can help the young parrot gain independence.

Many juvenile greys do not want to eat when left alone with food. The bird might wait until someone is around to point out the food and to model eating it before it will even seem to notice that there is food in the bowl. An older grey with more confidence will be more likely to overcome this inhibition, but a juvenile bird will often prefer to wait until the more-social activity of group feeding takes place.

Greys that have not been taught independence are much more likely to develop phobic behaviors and problems such as feather disorders. With guidance, even older birds can learn independence and will be better off if they do. Independent birds and their owners better enjoy the time they spend together because both humans and bird are calmer and more predictable.

**Note:** Watch the newly weaned juvenile carefully to determine whether or not it's eating. Occasionally, a newly weaned grey parrot might stop eating and beg incessantly as a reaction to the stress of moving. Breeders mention this in their instructions to new owners and suggest bringing the bird back for a few days for resocialization. Many breeders with closed aviaries won't allow the bird's return, but will suggest telephone support and will answer questions about whether the bird's failure to eat is physical or behavioral.

## Begging Behaviors

Learned, regressed, or retained begging behaviors are occasionally seen in grey parrots. The crying and begging postures might indicate that the bird wasn't fully weaned, they might indicate that the bird regressed to an unweaned state, or they might mean something else entirely.

Our first concern is physical health. A newly weaned juvenile parrot is a fragile creature and can quickly succumb to illness. (A sudden physical decline, which might take only hours, is called "crashing.") A bird that was fully weaned, then suddenly discontinues eating, could be demonstrating a physical response to illness. If the weaned juvenile has not already been seen by an avian veterinarian by the time

*This "begging" posture may be accompanied by begging cries.*

the crying problem appears, it should be taken to one as quickly as possible.

Occasionally, the young bird might be eating sufficiently when humans aren't there. Evaluate this possibility by weighing the bird the first thing every morning. An electronic scale that measures weight in grams is invaluable for this process. Keep a chart. If a healthy juvenile bird is losing weight, then we can presume that it is not getting sufficient nutrition. If the bird is being offered a healthy balanced diet, we must also presume that this bird is not eating independently.

**Food to offer:** Whether for reasons of health or behavior, juvenile grey parrots need warm food immediately, first thing after being weighed every morning. Offer warm baby formula, warm oatmeal, warm nutritious whole grain toast, or chunky warm food such as cooked pasta or sweet potatoes every morning before the begging starts. If you can get the food into the bird before the behavior begins, the behavior often will disappear immediately.

If the hand-feeder was using a dependable, balanced formula, try offering what the hand-feeder was feeding. Otherwise, try to find some Harrison's Bird Diet (available through a veterinarian) or other balanced and respected avian formula. Moisten the Harrison's cubes and offer them wet and warm, 100 to 105°F (37.8 to 40.6°C), one at a time, from the hand. When offering vegetables such as fresh or thawed frozen mixed vegetables to the baby parrot, try sprinkling the warm, moist vegetable mixture with a little Harrison's Juvenile Hand-feeding Formula. The hand-feeding formula increases the protein and other important nutrients missing in the vegetables, and the wet mixture served warm probably resembles chunky premasticated (chewed) food from the parents.

*Do not heat any parrot's food in a microwave oven.* Undetected hot spots develop that can burn the bird. Even professional hand-feeders are best advised not to use microwave ovens for the heating of parrot food.

Any parrot, but especially a young bird, will more willingly accept warm food than food at room temperature or cold. Jean Pattison suggests that giving a bird only a few bites of warm food from the hand can stimulate the bird to be interested in food in the bowl.[1] Some birds will also want or may prefer a warm meal before bedtime.

## Unintentional Reinforcement

Mother parrots snuggle, cuddle, and feed their babies when they are small, but once the babies are expected to learn to eat independently, their mother tries to redirect them to independent eating or other behaviors when they beg. Maturing neonates and juveniles turn to peers for allopreening and snuggling. Normal companion parrot babies also learn many other behaviors such as playing with toys, shredding toys, flapping, peek-a-boo, and vocal games. If they go to a new home during the developmental stage in which they are looking for peers to preen and to play with, they won't be as likely to fall back into begging behaviors.

**1.** Give active constructive attention to a begging bird so that it might learn more appropriate behavior.

**2.** Demonstrate independent eating by eating and offering to share food.

**3.** Initiate allopreening by gently scratching the jawbone, lores, ears, and nape.

**4.** Play with the bird with food toys when it's hungry.

**5.** Save those cuddles for evenings and naptimes and for occasional reassurance when confronted with unfamiliar (scary) things.

Juvenile grey parrots know they don't know what's best for them. They sit around flapping and looking expectant and waiting for someone to show them what to do. If the only coaching they have is how to cuddle, then cuddling is the only thing they will learn. In order to help the bird develop independent behaviors, including independent eating, owners should involve the baby in playing with toys, vocal "duets," climbing, exercising, shredding, and showering.

**Remember:** If the caretaker does not shape the bird's behavior, the bird will begin shaping the caregiver's behavior. This is generally not to the parrot's benefit. Indepen-

*Food "toys" can be given to a young grey that is begging for interaction.*

dence and confidence are much easier to instill if behavioral training is begun within a few weeks of the bird's arrival.

# Making the Most of the Early Days

Along with hope and anticipation, new owners often feel nervous, or maybe a little scared. They have just found the parrot of their dreams, and they don't want to do anything that might ruin its personality. However, with sensitive basic training and plenty of patience, both parrot and owner should enjoy a long life in each other's company.

The first days or weeks in the new home are the opportunity for humans to easily reinforce acceptable behavior, and establish the security that the parrot will base its self-confidence on. A well-planned environment, in which everyone consistently interacts with the bird and reinforces the bird's best responses, will enable the grey parrot's personality to blossom and allow the bird to explore different relationships with the members of its new flock.

A juvenile grey will feel more secure when it understands that its new keepers are predictable and trustworthy. Step-up practice and using labels or cues can establish predictability in the environment. Hands-on interactions such as the towel game can make the young parrot feel safe.

## Towel Technique

A bright-eyed young grey, brimming over with curiosity, will want to explore new things to the point of being almost afraid; then it will want to hide its head in a safe spot until it is sure there is nothing to be afraid of and curiosity kicks in again. Baby greys naturally feel safe in small dark areas with other warm bodies close by. To help reinforce curiosity and security, this is the perfect time to introduce the towel game.

Either a neonate or recently weaned juvenile can be carried around nestled in the loose folds of a towel as one might carry a kitten or a baby doll. The young bird will enjoy familiar or unfamiliar surroundings from this ultra-safe vantage point. When it's fun for the bird, the towel becomes a very useful tool for several aspects of parrot ownership:

*The towel game can increase feelings of confidence and security as well as reduce stress during trips to the veterinarian.*

**1.** Begin with a large towel or small blanket draped over your lap with the long ends hanging down on each side. Both size and color can be important. A too-small towel or a brightly colored or striped towel might not offer an appropriate sense of safety for some birds and many birds are afraid of the stripes. The most dependable early results will probably come from a gray towel the same color as the bird. Avoid knitted or crocheted Afghans as their loose threads can easily entrap little toes and cause panic. Also, examine the towel first and trim away any loose threads.

**2.** Put the bird on your lap and put one hand under each end of the towel. Lift the ends up to a point where the bird feels comfortable with it. Some greys will obviously prefer the ends high, making a sort of canyon or cavern inside the towel; others will prefer that the hands stay lower.

**3.** Eventually, sometimes right away, you can drape each end of the towel over the bird. Start looking for the bird and playing "Peek-a-bird." Most young greys will be calm and receptive to cuddling, head scratching, and feet rubbing during these interactions. Within a short time, you should be able to cover only the bird's head with the towel and it will allow petting of any place that is known to be enjoyable. (Favorite places often include the neck, nostrils, top of the head, around the eyes, the wing pit, and the hollow under the mandible.)

### Ernie or the Toweling Tale

Lucy acquired Ernie, a juvenile Red-tailed grey, from a breeder who had been unable to sell him at weaning. His social needs had been neglected; the breeder was busy feeding smaller babies and Ernie had become quite fearful. Lucy had the bird for about six months, and things were only getting worse. It seemed that they had no interactions that were pleasant for either of them. Lucy was close to giving up. Ernie's beak had gotten very sharp and Lucy, having been bitten badly on a number of occasions, was as afraid of Ernie as he was of everything.

Visiting a local bird store, Lucy remarked that she wished her grey would act like these. Someone who could help overheard.

Wrapping Ernie in a towel, they petted him and gently groomed the sharp tip of his beak with an emery board so that Lucy didn't have to be afraid of bleeding from a bite (again). Instead of taking Ernie out of the towel, Lucy sat on the floor with him wrapped up on her lap while talking to him. Pretty soon she was petting him, and he was enjoying it.

Gradually Lucy unwrapped Ernie. Within a couple of hours, Ernie was sitting on Lucy's hand and doing his first step-up training. In those short hours Lucy had made more progress in her relationship with Ernie than in the six months they had lived together!

*Many greys enjoy step-up practice as a bonding time.*

for grooming. Sometimes early reactions to too-aggressive or ill-planned toweling techniques can traumatize a bird so badly that its disposition is damaged. Early conditioning to enjoy the towel game will enable the young grey parrot to happily allow towel restraint. With good technique, even older greys that have not been programmed to be deathly afraid of towels can respond well to the towel game, by teaching the bird to be aware of the safety provided by a towel and by keeping a towel handy, you can provide a sense of safety any time and any place.

## Specialized Step-up Practice

African grey parrots seem to expect each person they meet to be different and to be able to form relationships with different people. Consistent handling, such as step-up practice (see page 11), helps to establish a basis for trusting everyone involved in the flock. There is a matter of people-training here, as allowing untrained humans to handle a sensitive young bird in unfriendly or provocative ways can cause the bird to bite or to become fearful.

The goal of patterning exercises is not to maintain dominant status with a grey; step-ups and other cued interactions are cooperation exercises intended to build and maintain trust. Early step-ups are best practiced in unfrequented territory, away from the cage, for a minute or so a couple of times daily, and ended after a successful interaction.

There is no wrong way to play the towel game if the bird is enjoying the process. A fun way to start with a bird that is unaccustomed to it is to let the bird see you playing it with another person or pet first. Greys are always tempted to join in when they see a "rival" having fun and getting attention. When there are two people, place a large towel on the bed. Take turns lifting up corners and "hiding" under the towel. Cover small pieces of a favorite food with a layer of towel. Whoever uncovers it first gets to eat it.

The interaction is similar to playing "Peek-a-boo" under the covers. (Cavity breeders spend a great deal of time in small places peeking out.) Many greys will engage in this activity once they know how much fun it is.

Throughout its lifetime, a parrot must submit to being restrained in a towel for veterinary examination or

Do not encourage or allow anyone to wave fingers in the bird's face or to provoke the bird by poking at it with inanimate objects. Nothing could be worse for the bird's disposition. If the bird is resisting patterning by a less-favored person, then the favorite person can participate more fully in step-up practice. This practice must be discontinued if it stimulates either aggression or fearfulness; don't do anything that causes the bird either to bite or to be afraid.

### Huey and the Step-up Story

Marci had been diligently practicing step-ups and the towel game to get her Red-tailed grey, Huey, through a very shy period. Huey's favorite toy was Blue Block, a piece of blue pine with a hole through it. Huey always had this toy with him.

One afternoon, Marci heard Huey saying "Step-up!" "Step-up!" repeatedly.

She saw Huey putting Blue Block on a perch.

Blue Block would fall off the perch, and Huey would say "Step-up!" and put it back again.

Finally Huey balanced Blue Block on the perch and announced, "Good Bird!"

While the step-up practice had seemed to be helping Huey, Marci was concerned that Huey might not be enjoying it. Now it was obvious that he was enjoying it, since he was using it as a self-rewarding (fun) behavior.

## Removing Your Bird from the Cage

Once your bird enjoys and cooperates with step-ups away from the cage, it can be stepped up from the cage top or the cage door. Because of their shy nature, grey parrots benefit from knowing that they are totally safe and in charge of their own cages when they are in their cages. Rather than expecting the bird to step up from inside the cage, let the bird choose whether to come out or not. Offer food "bribes" and encouragement, but don't forcibly remove a juvenile grey parrot; it may have a perfectly good reason to want to stay in the cage at that time (see Feather Development, page 51). This behavior will pass, usually within two to three weeks. If the bird establishes a pattern of not coming out at all, seek professional behavioral assistance.

## Other Socialization Processes

From the grey parrot's first days in the home, encourage the bird to remain open and accepting of relationships with several individuals. During the first months in the home, this should be rather easy, for, as we have previously observed, well-socialized juvenile greys are usually ready, willing, and able to form relationships with different people. If the bird is reluctant to interact with multiple individuals we might pattern with out-of-territory interactions such as step-ups, rescues, and outings (see page 123). However, interactions should not be forced. It's not unusual for a young bird to feel the need to solidify a predictable relationship with the most favored person before exploring relationships with others. The baby days are also the best time to train the bird to depend on humans for transportation from one bird-approved place to another.

A grey parrot, whether it's a baby or an adult is more likely to stay tame if it is handled every day of its entire life. Love, cuddling, and playing the towel game at least once each week will pattern the bird to intimate and restrictive handling. Many, but not all, companion greys like to be petted on the neck as do many other parrots, but most baby greys like to be hugged or snuggled.

Remember to facilitate, encourage, and reinforce the development of curiosity. Encourage the bird to

*Greys need to be handled every day.*

play independently by your side rather than demanding face-to-face interactions with humans every moment. Carefully reinforce appropriate intellectual exploration, as a grey may become protective of certain items, such as a food dish, a favorite toy, or a chrome appliance. If a grey is protecting an area or object, step the bird up onto a hand-held perch or allow it to leave the protected area before picking it up.

To avoid frightening the bird, maintain eye contact with your nose pointed away from the bird and only one eye visible to the bird. A baby grey that knows you're watching is less likely to act up; it may give little pinches to regain your attention.

## Establishing Cues: The Power of Suggestion

During this usually peaceful time, it is especially easy to teach a juvenile grey the meaning of the words "*Good bird*." Use these words of reinforcement generously. Birds also love to hear "*Pretty bird*" and "*I love you*." They enjoy the sounds of these words and phrases when spoken with enthusiasm. Demonstrating affection with these words provides a valuable precedent for maintaining good behaviors in the future.

If the bird knows that good things come to good birds, we can use these positive words as cues to suggest appropriate behavior. This is more effective than the use of "*No*" or "*Don't*" or "*Stop*," which might temporarily interrupt a bird whose heart is set on doing something—

such as biting someone—but they won't necessarily prevent the behavior. If we say, instead, "*Be a good bird*," we remind the bird of those good things that come to good birds, and we are more likely to have guided the bird to appropriate behavior, not merely caused hesitation. This can be a tremendously powerful tool during the coming developmental period and beyond.

## Submission Patterning

Playing games where submissive behavior is rewarded also helps to prevent biting. As with other patterning strategies, the bird's enjoyment of the process is crucial to the success of the practice.

Many people report being able to restrain a nipping or potentially nipping grey parrot gently by the maxilla, between the thumb and the knuckle of the index finger, then kissing it on the forehead. Another similar technique involves holding the bird's head in the same way one would simultaneously caress the top and bottom of the head, and kissing the top of the maxilla. Careful and sensitive restraint of the use of the beak is necessary here. Many of the birds will learn to vocalize a "smack" or other expression of joy that comes with the smack of the human kiss. This type of human/parrot kissing is safe for both humans and bird.

These techniques are effective only if the bird has learned to enjoy them before they are used to address a problem. A similar strategy involves teaching the bird to dis-

*Some greys enjoy playing on their backs.*

continue a particular behavior by using a stern, straight-on gaze and the cue, "*Be careful*." The setup goes like this: When the juvenile bird is about to experience something you know it will dislike—whether that's falling off a swing or a chewed perch or losing its grip on a hand—say to the bird "*Be careful*."

The bird can easily learn that "*Be careful*" means that something is going to happen that it doesn't want to happen. Practice giving the bird a stern look with eyes wide open in order to convey a sense of limits. However, straight-on eye contact may be too threatening for a shy or phobic juvenile grey, as it resembles the stalking gaze of a predator. With a very shy young grey, even a stern look might have to be delivered with only one eye (see page 121).

In the future you will be able to deliver that stern look to the bird from across the room and say *"Be careful"* when you want to interrupt an unwanted behavior. The interruption you provide may be brief. Sometimes, reminding the bird to be a good bird is sufficient to stimulate different behavior, but other times, you will also have to go over and move the bird in order to physically prevent the behavior.

## Occasional Nipping Behaviors

During these precious early days in the home, nips should be rare and experimental. The very best way to deal with occasional nips and pinches is to avoid situations where they occur and to simply ignore them. Remember that most behaviors that are not reinforced will probably disappear.

Humans must not take it personally when a juvenile grey experiments on flesh with its beak. The young parrot must be handled in ways in which nipping is not possible so that these behaviors cannot be repeatedly enacted and inadvertently reinforced into patterns. This means not putting fingers in front of the beak. When stepping-up, announce the interaction, then move your hand over the feet from below. When petting the neck, hold the bird close so it has the opportunity to press its face into the security of a shirt while the hand approaches. A

grey might love being scratched, but a hand coming toward the head can be scary enough to provoke a nip.

## An Understanding of Time

A bird inhabiting a controlled environment never sees the shadows grow long, then short, then long, or hears the frogs start croaking exactly 30 minutes before sundown. An indoor bird never knows the heat of the noonday sun followed by cooling afternoon showers. These are all natural cycles that enable a wild bird to easily perceive the passage of time.

We can include environmental elements that demonstrate the passage of time—a singing bird clock, a full-spectrum light that comes on and goes off every day at the same time, or a television that is set to come on at the same time with the same program every day for regular TV time.

Establishing time markers in the indoor environment is helpful in conditioning a grey parrot to tolerate being "abandoned" during the day. That is, if the bird is accustomed to having an in-home companion all day, and that companion then goes to work outside the home, the bird might develop adverse behavioral reactions related to feeling abandoned. If TV time is well established before any radical schedule changes are made, the bird will not usually react negatively to other changes. TV time will be a constant in an ever-changing world. The presence of these types of constants helps the bird to tolerate changes.

# Grey Parrots with Children and Other Pets

Grey parrots have not been traditionally considered well suited as companions for children. In the past decade, as they have become increasingly adapted to domestic breeding, the birds have changed. The new generations of greys are more likely to adapt well to children and vice versa. There is great potential for highly complimentary relationships between African greys and children, especially between an only African grey and an only child. There is also potential for children to damage the sensitive African grey personality, and there is potential for a grey parrot's sharp beak to damage a sensitive child's skin and personality.

The best candidates for juvenile African grey owners are kind children who are at least eight to ten years old. Of course, this advice is highly subjective and depends completely upon the bird and the child. Some young children are able to develop and maintain excellent relationships with African grey parrots. One two-year-old might do very well with a particular grey parrot, and a teenager might not do well with the very same bird.

Careful training of children to perform the towel game, step-up practice, and adult supervision of the development of the relationship are necessary to ensure a peaceful African grey/child relationship. The bird must be patterned to demonstrate the same cooperative behaviors with the child as it would with its parent. It is especially important to teach a child not to chase a frightened African grey parrot that is running away. A child who chases a fearful grey parrot can provoke the fight-or-flight response in the bird, fear biting, defensive aggression, or ongoing panic behaviors. If the African grey runs away from the child, train the child to wait until the bird gets to a corner or stopping place, then the child should approach slowly and give the step-up command, either with a hand-held perch, a bare hand, or a hand covered by a towel in preparation for the towel game. If the bird does not calm down and readily comply with the child's step-up prompt, or if the bird continues in panic mode, instruct the child to seek adult assistance in returning a sense of safety to the bird.

A child must be able to expect help and support from adults in providing adequate care, including annual veterinary exams, for any companion animal. Adults should also regularly examine and trim wing feathers to prevent the loss of the bird from flying-related accidents.

**Important:** Children should be supervised, counseled, and reminded to leave the toilet lid down so that the bird will not drown in the toilet. Likewise, everyone must be vigilant not to leave glasses with liquid where the bird has access to this common drowning hazard. Children must not

*When introducing a new bird to the family, pay attention to the original parrot first.*

sleep with these friendly birds and must also be careful not to close them into drawers and doors.

## Introducing a New Baby to an Established Grey Parrot

Any significant changes are best approached gradually if possible. A new baby entering the home falls into this category. Jealousy cannot be completely avoided; however, the stress of the situation can be lessened with careful planning.

Providing the grey parrot with a schedule of attention it can count on can help the bird to feel secure. Months before the baby arrives, you can set aside a specific time of the day that will be devoted to playing with the bird. This can occur at a specific time in the day's routines. Following this pattern as closely as possible after the baby arrives will help the bird know that it isn't being forgotten.

Once the baby arrives, it will be a sudden dominating force in the lives of the parents. This change can be made gradually with the introduction of a baby doll. The expecting parents can first play with the bird, then play with the baby doll. Playing with the bird for a short while after the doll is put away can help the bird realize it is still an important part of your life. This doll play can be done occasionally at first and then with increasing frequency as the baby's arrival date approaches. The companion grey must understand that it is not to touch the baby and should not learn to expect to interact with the new child.

Once the baby is home, using the bird's name in tandem with the baby's name, as in *"Jaco's Justin"* and *"Justin's Jaco,"* can reinforce the connection between the bird and the baby. Once the bird sees that the baby gets immediate attention when it cries, a grey parrot will probably learn to cry like the baby. Ignoring the bird's crying is probably the best course of action, as any response will reinforce the behavior. The bird will usually stop on its own once the baby stops crying so much. If the noise competition between the baby and the bird becomes problematic, this might be a nice time for the bird to go for an extended visit in a loving foster home.

## Other Pets

African greys may develop extremely compatible relationships with other pets; they also might develop highly adversarial relationships with them. Like other parrots, African greys often violently defend a bond to a location or a human and jealously abuse others, including pets, that might be perceived as intruders into their territory. While the adjustment period is crucial, some animals will never be able to be together without strict supervision. Here are some guidelines:

• Prepare to introduce a new pet into the home of an established African grey in much the same way as preparing for a new human baby, by telling the bird that the new addition is coming and by sensitively supervising their introduction. You can help the introduction along by introducing the bird first to the accessories needed by the new addition; for instance, let the bird chew on the new dog's collar or the new cat's toys. Use the bird's name in tandem with the new creature: *"Dakar's puppy is coming!" "Does the puppy's Dakar want a treat?"*

• Although a grey parrot is much more likely to be killed by a dog than by a cat, caring owners know that their cats must be well socialized as kittens. Some owners even feel that a cat's front claws should be removed if there is a bird in the house. When supervising a new African grey/dog or cat relationship, a carefully timed clap, squirt, or tap on the predator animal's too-interested nose may pattern small pet mammals to discontinue stalking a bird. Always intervene if either animal seems to be trying to chase or attack.

• Always play with the established grey parrot first. Greys don't usually provoke other animals as much as smaller birds such as *Brotegeris* or *Poicephalus*, but jealousy can do strange things, and an African grey can be extremely defensive of favorite people, toys, or locations. If a particular bird decides that harassing the dog is necessary, you can no longer trust that bird with that dog. If the bird has abused the dog repeatedly in the past, some day that dog will defend itself, and the bird might not survive.

• Locating the cage well away from traffic areas is important, for a sense of safety. If boisterous animals frequently rush past the grey parrot cage, the bird might develop aggression, fail to talk, begin fraying feathers, or develop thrashing or other problematic behaviors.

• While most African greys share homes well with most cats, ferrets are especially deadly even to larger birds. We do not recommend adding an African grey or any other parrot to a home with a free-roaming ferret.

• African greys can be surprisingly accepting of new birds, although it varies from bird to bird. Many grey parrots cannot be trusted with either larger or smaller birds. Carefully supervise any interaction in which a larger animal interacts with a smaller one, especially if the African grey is the larger animal. African greys can be a threat to smaller creatures such as insects, spiders, lizards, reptiles, mice, hamsters, and gerbils.

# The Previously Owned Grey Parrot

An adoption or resale grey parrot with good companion potential is probably a domestic bird that is no more than three to six years old. A grey parrot that has not been handled might be either aggressive or terrified (or sometimes both), but moving the bird will make a noticeable difference. Maladjusted grey parrots often respond positively to being moved, and a new home often brings radically improved behavior almost spontaneously.

### Ways to Help the New Bird Adjust

Most grey parrots are cautious, and changing homes can be unsettling. Every effort should be made to help the bird feel safe. It's probably a good idea to leave a towel or blanket, being careful of strings that might trap little toenails, over at least half the cage for the first few days. Try setting the cage at chest level first, and if the bird seems nervous, try either raising or lowering the cage until the bird seems more at ease. If there are no other established birds in the living area, situate the new grey in the living area, but well out of traffic areas.

The changes encountered when coming to a new home usually provide a temporary window of opportunity for reinforcing good behavior. This is similar to the "honeymoon period" experienced by baby hand-feds coming into the first home, but the window of good behavior may be very brief. Work quickly and consistently to make the most of this fleeting opportunity.

### Rehabilitation

An adoption grey may not have had the best care, so begin rehabilitation by taking the bird immediately to an avian veterinarian, possibly even before taking the bird home. Be sure to observe appropriate quarantine procedures as specified by the veterinarian, especially if there are other birds in the home. This period will probably be at least one to three months, during which time the new parrot must be behaviorally rehabilitated. If behavioral rehabilitation is not begun until after quarantine, you may have already missed the window of opportunity to easily reinforce appropriate behavior. Ask the veterinarian to examine and update the bird's wing feather trim. This is important in training or retraining the bird to step-ups.

### Interactions

Begin interactions with a wary bird by playing eye games and approaching with nonthreatening posture. It is best to establish contact with the bird first with games involving no eye contact and progress to games involving limited eye contact (see Guide to Games page 120).

If the bird can be handled and is not too frightened, hold it as much as possible during the first 48 hours in the new home. If it can be accomplished productively, work on step-up patterning (see page 11) for as long as you and the bird seem to enjoy doing it. Try to be nurturing, supportive, and consistent. Handle the bird less if it seems to tire easily, perhaps providing a little extra heat and sleep time for the first few days.

Even though the relocated bird should have no strongly developed instincts to defend new territory, be sure to practice step-ups in a contained area outside the bird's new home territory. Be sure also to pattern the bird to step up onto a hand-held perch as well as onto hands. The bird may be reluctant to step up from the cage, so don't attempt step-ups from the cage unless the bird is first well patterned to step-ups in unfamiliar territory.

A young resale domestic bird should be socialized exactly as a baby grey would be. A two-to-three-year-old grey parrot in a new home should go through a "honeymoon period" similar to the baby days, followed by the "terrible twos" (see page 164), just as a baby bird would, but these developmental phases will be of much shorter duration with the older bird.

## Diet

When the bird's diagnostic tests come back, ask the veterinarian before trying to improve the bird's diet by supplementing vitamins. If the

*Adopting an older grey can be a rewarding experience.*

bird has a less-than-healthy liver or kidneys, be very careful about vitamin supplementation, especially with $D_3$, which could kill the bird. Better to improve diet with real food: Fresh fruits, vegetables, pasta, and a quality commercial diet (see Diet, page 80). Almost any food—quality whole grain toast, macaroni and cheese, or oatmeal—served warm should seem like love to a previously hand-fed grey that has been neglected. A grey parrot that is responding to the love inspired by warm food will probably want to feed you.

It's not unusual for a newly adopted grey to prefer to eat nothing but seeds, especially sunflower or safflower seeds. This is similar to adopting a child who will eat only french fries. Put these birds on a canary-based mix as quickly as possible, then you can begin familiarizing the bird with a pelleted diet.

*The very important task of getting an older grey to eat a healthy diet can be a challenge.*

Eventually wean the bird to the pelleted diet.

## Socializing

As quickly as possible, the bird should be socialized to enjoy the towel game (see page 30). A bird that has been mishandled may be terrified of the towel. Be sure to use a solid-color towel with no stripes, as many grey parrots are frightened of towels with stripes. Try to use a towel that is the same color as the bird. The goal here is to replicate the feeling of security of being under Mommy's wings. If the bird is initially afraid of the towel, try playing with the bird in the covers of the bed. Blankets may be less intimidating to a bird that has been roughly toweled. But be sure not to fall asleep when playing snuggle games with the bird in the bed.

# The Wild-caught Grey

The last legal wild-caught grey parrots entered the United States in 1992. During the last decade of importation, many of these birds were so calm and came in so close to tame that many people suspected that they were being captive-bred rather than captured. In many cases, the only way to identify a resocialized wild-caught grey from a resocialized hand-fed is by the open band. Many of these birds have made premium companions. If these birds live to their 50s or 60s, there will be older wild-caught grey parrots occasionally available in the United States through the middle of this century.

Although older and possibly never before socialized to human touch, for a person with great patience, these birds can offer good companion potential. These birds require the same veterinary examination and quarantine as other birds. They may experience stages of behavioral development similar to those of a domestic baby parrot as they acclimate to the new home. Similar behavioral strategies and socialization processes as with hand-feds are used, but changes must be made more slowly, with this exception: A new hand-fed grey parrot baby should be held for limited periods only, guiding it to learn to play alone (develop independence). An older, bird-bonded or wild-caught grey parrot can be held for long periods of time to build and improve the human/grey bond if the bird is enjoying the interaction.

# Aviary Birds

Just as there are grey parrots that prefer to live with humans, there are grey parrots that prefer to live with birds. A bird may be so bonded to its wild roles, so intent on its own personal motivations, that it is completely unable to live with humans. Every moment in the company of humans can represent life-threatening stress to such a bird. Every effort should be made to provide the bird with as natural an environment as possible, with an attempt being made to shield this bird from contact with humans.

[1] Jean Pattison, Interview, October, 1998.

## Chapter Three

# Ongoing Behavior Management

## The Developmental Period

**B**etween four and twenty-four months, a juvenile grey is carefully studying its surroundings and the behaviors of its "flockmates." What it learns during this time, along with inherited traits, will combine to form the individual's personality. The bird's curiosity is budding; it's developing confidence that it will need for the rest of its life. It is picking up cues from its environment and is developing relationships with its companions, feathered or not. It's finding its status in the flock.

While younger greys might solicit attention from anyone, maturing juveniles become more discriminatory about who holds, and therefore, controls them. In nature, flocks with the strongest members live longer and have more babies. Young parrots survive by studying the more confident members of the flock and copying their behavior. These individuals have proved their prowess and earned the respect of others. The birds also watch weaker mem-

bers and distance themselves from individuals that might jeopardize the well-being of the flock.

In the wild or in the living room, a juvenile grey will place more trust in individuals it perceives to be stronger or more fit. The bird might judge a person by the self-confidence projected or by an event in which the person proved to be worthy or unworthy. During the Developmental Period, a juvenile grey is likely to test the person in order to form a judgment. Of course, this test often involves use of the beak. Judgments it makes or grudges it develops during this stage may last a very long time.

In the wild these juvenile birds would be busily learning survival skills. They would be following adult flock members around, mimicking their actions. Avoiding predators is one of those skills. If the young grey comes to view humans as predators because of a frightening incident, for example, it can't help but try to avoid humans. If a human picks up a grey while it is panicking, the bird might associate that person with being afraid, possibly viewing that person in the same light that it might view a predator. The parrot might then bite that person out of fear. Fear bites are much harder than bites intended to cause fear.

# Transitional Behaviors

**Nippy stages:** Grey owners frequently report that their birds go through nippy stages during the first years in the home. This experimental nipping is normal behavioral development as a well-adjusted grey begins showing signs of the strength of personality and independence necessary to be an adult. If the bird has been carefully guided to develop confidence, the grey in this phase might be a contrary and determined creature similar to a human child in the "terrible twos." The bird will be increasingly exploratory and experimental. This behavioral phase is both expected and beneficial. It should appear, at least momentarily, or there may be concern that the bird will not develop confidence.

**Shy stage:** Many grey owners also report that their birds go through a shy stage during this same period. In some birds, the nippy stage might be prominent; in some birds, the shy stage will be prominent. Either or both stages might appear suddenly but both stages might be virtually unnoticeable in a bird that is handled fre-

quently and socialized as suggested in this book.

Shyness can also disappear suddenly. A young grey parrot is probably stimulated to overcome shyness when it meets a potential mate. If a shy young grey has a "thunderbolt"—an immediate "matelike" attraction to a particular human—that impulse can be exploited, stimulated, and reinforced, and almost immediately, the bird can become less shy with everyone.

**Fight-or-flight:** During the Developmental Period we may see dramatic instinctual reactions to perceived danger. This fight-or-flight response is part of the bird's necessary survival mechanism in the wild. If a juvenile grey parrot was not previously well patterned, it risks losing confidence in the bond with humans. If patterned controls—step-ups, the

*Keeping a grey off the shoulder during its developmental period is a good idea.*

towel game, transportation dependence, and submissive interactions—are not in place, changes can appear swiftly.

A fight-or-flight response is significantly more intense that simply ducking into a corner. Once we see it, we must be careful not to frustrate or reinforce resulting behavior. Our experience suggests that the earlier a strong enactment of the fight-or-fight response (panic) appears, the more likely it is to be enduring. The enactment of a fight-or-flight response by a mature grey will probably be of more temporary duration than fearfulness developing in a grey parrot before one year of age.

# Helping the Bird Develop Self-confidence

A typical new parrot owner wants to provide the bird with everything it needs. To achieve this, the new owner might buy the best food, a nice cage, and lots of toys, and shower the bird with attention. However, as a wild animal, the African grey is designed to have to meet its own needs. Similar to humans, the parrot experiences stress when it doesn't feel able to do this or feels that it has little control over its life.

While other parrots will take a measure of control and are independent by nature, the grey has to be helped to realize this potential. During the Developmental Period, the young bird is an intellectual sponge. It craves learning how to explore, interact, and function on its own, and how to fit into the social group.

Exploring and playing are easy to encourage at this age. Provide a safe vantage point that the youngster can retreat to when feeling overwhelmed, either under a towel or blanket, in the crook of the arm, or in the lap. The bird can then be presented with opportunities to investigate. Both the person and the bird can get down on a blanket on the floor to play with a variety of toys together. The owner can demonstrate shredding and jangling while the baby watches to see if anything bad happens or if its role model is having fun. They can travel to new rooms in the house together and meet new people. Learning about these activities at this age allows the bird to entertain itself in the absence of flock members and allows it to keep its composure when scenery changes.

Feelings of involvement can be fostered by including the bird in what ordinarily would be flock activities. Responding to pleasant vocalizations will encourage talking and give the bird a chance to learn to ask for the things it needs. The bird will want to be included in mealtimes. It will need to be able to see when flock members are coming or going, and will want to participate in group activities even if that is watching television.

Consistent handling techniques and training procedures guide the bird to good behavior. The self-confidence the bird develops from learning to be both independent and a participating member of the family will ensure the bird's successful lifetime adjustment as a companion.

## Opportunities to Make Successful Decisions

In order to avoid the formation of phobias or fearfulness, young parrots must have opportunities to make successful decisions. In an inadequately designed environment, it's possible for a young parrot to find lots of unacceptable things to do, and Mom or Dad can wind up constantly retrieving the bird from inappropriate activities. Always thwarting the bird's budding curiosity can be damaging to a young parrot's behavior.

It's important, therefore, for a bird to have multiple appropriate options about how and where it spends its time and numerous toys to play with. Even if a bird chooses not to play on a particular perch, or if it decides not to play with a particular toy, the presence of the second toy or perch has provided an opportunity for successful decision making. The process enhances confidence.

## Testing Behaviors

Anyone wishing to handle a grey parrot must earn the bird's respect

*Including the parrot in daily activities helps build socialization skills and confidence.*

while keeping his or her skin intact. The first step is to maintain "grey-friendly" posture. A bird that feels threatened or defensive always bites harder. Body language that is interpreted as friendly to a grey includes moving the head forward and lower than usual. Squinting eyes slightly and looking sideways at the bird will also be interpreted as friendly. Making a long, low, "*Helloooo*" sound or a clucking or knocking noise with the tongue also helps maintain a friendlier level of interaction. These gestures can be incorporated into the routine step-up practices and the daily practice of getting the bird out of the cage. Every time you respond to the grey in a friendly and predictable manner, you are building trust.

When approaching the bird with your hand for it to step up on, you

*Diverse textures and toys give young greys the opportunity to make successful decisions.*

announce your intentions before offering your hand to the bird. Saying *"Step up"* first and then again as you place your hand near the bird's feet allows the parrot to adjust to what is going to happen. A grey is much more cooperative if it is not caught off guard. If the bird reaches for your fingers with its beak, say nothing, but move your hand toward the bird's chest until the bird lets go. You can then continue moving your hand toward the bird's feet to get it to step up.

Young birds might have difficulty containing their enthusiasm while being handled. Gestures that begin affectionately may become painful as the bird's excitement overcomes it; therefore, it is best to simply stay out of the way of the beak. Affectionately restraining the head while petting is often effective in distracting the bird and can enable it to regain self-control. Ideally, provide an alternative object for the bird to chew. Especially, if the bird is focused on chewing its "perch" (the hand it's standing on), it may be provided with a small "holding" toy to chew instead.

### Distracting from a Bite

As the bird's behavior becomes increasingly experimental, it might become necessary to respond a little more directly to test nips that occur during step-up practice. First be sure to offer your hand properly, coming from below and just over the feet near the place where the leg joins the belly. Be sure to maintain eye contact and don't look at the approaching hand. Then, if the bird nips the hand you offer, quickly dip the ends of the fingers of the hand the bird is sitting on—not the hand you are offering—and return the hand to its former position. This must be accomplished carefully so that the grey parrot does not fall or become fearful during the process.

The bird must discontinue the nip in order to regain balance. It will soon realize that nips during step-ups cause it to lose balance. This distraction device is a small wobble. It must be done quickly, gently, and sensitively in combination with suggesting appropriate behavior such as *"Be careful"* or *"Be a good bird,"* so that the bird is not too affected either physically or emotionally. This technique is not a patterning device to be used frequently, but rather a technique that is used only occasionally to distract the bird from unwanted behavior.

# Manipulating the Perception of Territory

If a grey is increasingly showing territorial-related aggression, try rearranging and moving the cage and play areas. Occasional outings where the bird is handled by sensitive, astute strangers can be used to manipulate excessive bonding tendencies, improve patterning, and minimize territorialism. Don't forget the importance of a separate roost/cage and foraging territories such as a play area or second cage, and the role of transportation dependence—carrying the bird from one area to the other—in maintaining cooperative behavior.

Of course, one bird might need more careful patterning, while another might need more stimulating activities, and still another bird might absolutely *have* to have a bath every day. Be alert to averting behavioral problems by anticipating your bird's physical and emotional needs. Negative behaviors evolving during the Developmental Period can be lasting.

# Accidental Reinforcement of Unwanted Behaviors

If your skin becomes too closely involved with the inside of a bird's beak, the bird is testing to decide how to view you. Pulling away and yelling "*Ouch! Bad bird!*" is a clear message that you are not establishing the rules. This can be uncomfortable for a grey in the Developmental Period. A bird at this age is not ready to be dominant over humans and will not feel secure in that role. The young parrot's reaction might be to bite harder the next time you approach, and subsequent bites will have much more behind them than just a test. The bird is displaying insecurity, sometimes to the point of fear, and frustration at being put in a position it isn't yet ready to handle.

An older bird might take this opportunity to take control of the situation and accept that this weak human should be aggressively pushed away from the strong flock whenever given the chance. For a young grey there may be a fear response mixed in. If you continue to back down from the bird, the bird may actually become afraid of you. Because fearful greys have a much harder bite, these frightened birds are often labeled as mean or even vicious. The more often you try unsuccessfully to handle a frightened bird, the more afraid the bird will become.

To break this cycle, you must immediately stop trying to handle the bird. Repeatedly forcing unsuccessful interaction can cause a grey parrot to hold one of the grudges these birds are notorious for. Whenever moving forward fails, it's time to move back to successful interactions, sometimes back to the beginning of the relationship. If the bird has been spooked enough to not want to come out of the cage, then you must use friendly postures and talk to the bird through the bars. The bird can begin to get used to your hands being in sight or resting on the cage. It must get used to the cage door being open. Patiently allow the bird to choose when it wants to come out of the cage.

It's not unusual for a caregiver to shower affection and concern on a parrot that is acting afraid. If this happens a few times, the bird might then decide that the best way to get affection is to act afraid. The owner is generally better off letting the bird

*A grey displaying territorial aggression may need to be removed from the area with a hand-held perch.*

calm down alone and then providing attention and reassurance when the bird has regained composure. The towel game can also be used to reinforce security in a bird that is conditioned to the game.

If the bird is reacting fearfully, you can regain the parrot's respect with the help of another person. This person should be someone either the bird already trusts or someone who can easily win the bird's trust. This person can "reintroduce" you (see also Outings on page 123).

# Correcting Unacceptable Behaviors

The bird will test the limits of acceptable behavior by challenging the status and authority of "flock members" in other ways. You must correct annoying vocalizations, roaming, chasing, and any other unacceptable behaviors so that they will not become a permanent part of the bird's personality.

Successful patterning means frequent handling with no bites. Ineffective handling can sometimes be worse than no handling, but no handling is also bad during this period. If the bird is beginning to bite repeatedly during this period, use the towel game, interactive submissive postures, hand-held perches, or stop handling the bird, play eye games, and seek professional assistance right away.

# Feather Development and Related Behavior

Greys begin molting wing feathers at around 12 months old. Often, the first flight feathers to molt out are primaries near the end of the wing. Once the blood feathers reach a certain length they are fragile and sensitive. If the young bird's wing feathers have been trimmed, especially if those feathers were trimmed very short, the blood feather will have little

### Two-person Step-ups

When passing a grey to someone who the bird isn't sure it wants to go to, the trusted person holds the grey on the left hand. Using the right hand, this person takes hold of the right hand of the less-favored person, as if they were shaking hands, except that they don't let go. The trusted person then moves the bird toward the other person's arm, with the hand slightly lower than the arm, and suggests that the bird step up.

The bird may step on the other person's arm and walk directly over to the trusted person's arm; as long as the bird isn't jumping off, this is progress. Eventually, the trusted person's arm can be pulled away, leaving the bird on the less-favored person's arm. That person can now renew the emphasis on trust-winning exercises, such as step-up practice.

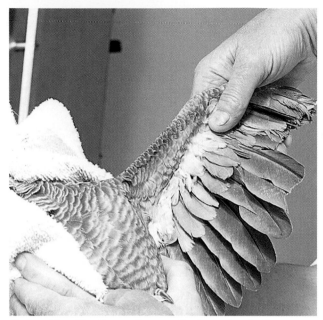

*Broken blood feathers often result when wing feathers are trimmed too short to provide the new feathers with protection as they regrow.*

protection and can break simply through the act of flapping the wings. Young greys will be more sensitive to protecting those feathers (for more on feathers, see page 128).

Often, young greys, between 12 and 18 months, will avoid any activity that involves flapping the wings if there are blood feathers in danger of breaking. This may mean that a bird might avoid coming out of the cage for two to three weeks while the blood feathers finish developing. If you insist that the bird come out of the cage anyway, the bird might become very nervous when you approach, although it may still tolerate handling by others. It is best to let the bird finish growing the feath-

ers, then if there are still problems handling the bird, they can be addressed when the parrot is out of danger of being physically (and as a result, emotionally) damaged.

# The Fickle Grey Parrot

Greys usually switch loyalties toward the end of the Developmental Period. The grey has changing needs to be met from a favored companion and is trying to meet those needs. A young grey wants to associate with someone strong. In the wild, the bird would use such a role model to help become a strong, successful, long-lived parrot. Toward the end of the Developmental Period, the bird may switch loyalties to someone it sees more as an equal. A grey parrot will probably not want a mate that will boss it around, nor does it want a mate that cannot stand up for itself.

To solidify a new mate-type relationship, the grey may feel compelled to push the former favorite person away. This is usually temporary. If the former favorite person can wait it out, he or she will regain the bird's acceptance, as long as that person hasn't pushed the grey to holding a grudge. Patience is the key. These birds are very social by nature and like to have many companions. They usually form relationships with everyone in the family, if they are given a chance.

# Maintaining Companion Behaviors as the Bird Matures

As the Developmental Period passes, the young grey parrot might become so cooperative that we are tempted to discontinue step-up practice and the towel game. This is not a good idea, even if the bird seems totally docile at this time. Usually, however, at least one nippy period will come and go between the Developmental Period and the appearance of sexually related behaviors that might be called adolescence.

The techniques described here are intended to enhance favorable behaviors in companion greys and to suppress or minimize most behaviors related to breeding. Some greys will be kept easily tame; some will be difficult. Expect every bird to be a little different, with vast differences between successfully socialized birds and unsocialized birds. If all interactions are consistent, the bird will be more predictable.

As breeding age approaches (see page 150), we will see heightened exploration and physical and emotional experimentation. The bird might change emotional and/or territorial loyalties, becoming aggressive around a newly-selected territory or a new favorite human (mate substitute).

It might be necessary to take an arrogant young grey out of its familiar territory for at least a few days each year in order to repattern the bird and to require interactions with unfamiliar humans. Vacations and indoor "outings" (visits to unfamiliar territory) are very helpful at this time. Even a simple car ride with the bird in a carrier can make a wonderful difference in a grey parrot's disposition. Careful transporting and meticulous wing feather trims will ensure safety on these outings.

As time passes, a grey parrot may become increasingly concerned with immediate environmental control. The bird might start attacking tissues, or people sneezing or blowing into tissues. It might also attack someone cleaning with quick motions using paper towels. A maturing grey might suddenly decide it loves, or hates, a particular dog or cat or stuffed animal.

If allowed a great deal of liberty in the home, the bird might become hypervigilant or aggressive around a suddenly and mysteriously selected territory. The maturing grey parrot will be seeking both companions and interlopers in its reflections.

There must be at least one enemy that can be regularly thwarted. To a very real extent, the bird must select or identify this enemy independently. Of course, it's very important for this enemy to not be a living creature or a treasured human possession, so several potential, approved surrogate enemies must be provided. Safe, unbreakable toys and loud, bird-safe bells are excellent candidates. If a young companion grey has no opportunity to release natural aggressive parrot energy, the bird is likely to begin to express that natural parrot energy against whatever or whomever is closest.

If the bird is enjoying attacking a toy, leave them both alone. The bird is unlikely to be cooperative at this time. There will continue to be many times when the bird will solicit human attention. It's best to handle the bird when the experience is more likely to be successful. The more successful behavioral experiences you have at this time, and the more the bird is patterned and reinforced to cooperate, the more likely the bird is to cooperate when it becomes fully mature.

## Chewing and Other Behaviors

By three years of age, a normal grey parrot will begin exhibiting some pretty impressive chewing behaviors. This is when the bird is starting to say to the world: "See what a good parent I could be!" As chewing behaviors develop, it's necessary to increase the number and frequency of chewables in the cage or the play area.

As with human children, new behaviors will seem to suddenly appear out of nowhere. For months, the bird will ignore the picture frame behind the cage. Then one day, the picture frame is a pile of splinters on the floor. For years, the bird might put nothing into its water, then one day it will begin filling the water bowl with debris. A maturing grey parrot might suddenly begin pulling newspaper up through the bottom grate.

All of these behaviors are part of the grey parrot's instinctive need to attract a suitable mate. An industrious mate is probably highly prized in

*A grey parrot might become protective of its cage.*

## "Good Hand/Bad Hand"

The maturing grey might begin to bite even a well-placed hand prompt for the step-up command. This might occur especially when the owner looks away or the bird is being removed from a familiar perch or top of the cage. Sometimes this behavior can be defeated with improved handling technique.

Maintain eye contact and offer the hand to be stepped on, approaching from below, as usual. Just as the prompt hand begins its approach to the bird, present an unfamiliar object in the bite zone with one hand and give the step-up command with the other hand, followed by "*Be a good bird*."

That is, if you want the bird to step-up, and it is threatening to bite the hand you want it to step on, pick up a small object such as a spoon or a piece of junk mail and hold it about an inch (2.5 cm) below and in front of the bird's beak, give

the "*Up*" command, and suggest good behavior. Usually the surprised bird, responding to the familiar behavioral pattern, and knowing what "*Good bird*" means, responds also by being what it is expected to be—a good bird.

**Eye contact:** Eye contact is especially important here. A bird will often maintain eye contact rather than bite. If the bird's eye is distracted by the introduced object, it will seek to regain eye contact immediately rather than take the time to bite after being distracted.

Even if the bird bites, that unfamiliar object, rather than the hand being offered, will be bitten. Take care that the distraction device is not frightening to a shy grey. The distraction object must be neither too large, which might scare the bird off the perch, too small, which might be ineffective, nor toxic as in the case of soap or a piece of lead or solder.

the wild. We can't punish a bird for chewing up things when it's doing its darndest to be the best that it can be. We must provide appropriate things to chew and reinforce the bird for chewing appropriately.

## Fearfulness

As grey parrots mature, they may become increasingly obsessed with control of their immediate environment. If they feel they have no con-

trol, or if they are repeatedly pushed in ways that stimulate and reinforce panic, they will become increasingly shy. If we see a trend of developing fearfulness, we must take action to improve the bird's confidence, perhaps allowing it to live higher—or lower, depending upon the bird—allowing it to occasionally choose whether to leave the cage on its own, or providing a place to hide. The addition of a small tent that is

*As a result of covering this grey's cage, he eventually gained enough confidence to come to the door instead of cowering in the back.*

open on two sides might be an excellent choice for a shy grey. It's not unusual to see a temporary increase in aggressive behaviors. In such a case, this is exactly what we want to see at this time.

## Sexual Maturity and Aggression

There will come a time when threats might be accompanied by aggression; a bite might actually break the skin. During this time it's not unusual for both predictable and unpredictable bites to occur, especially in the bird's perceived territory. Usually there will be plenty of warning: hypervigilance, eye movement, raised feathers across the shoulders or tops of wings, charging with beak open, or any other body language that usually accompanies aggression in this individual.

If a grey parrot has not been appropriately provided for until this time, attempts to socialize or resocialize may be met with great resistance from the bird.

The best way to deal with aggression appearing at sexual maturity, around six years, is to give the bird space to be obnoxious. That is not to say, reinforce obnoxious behavior. Never allow the grey parrot to chase or harass. Calmly remind the bird to "*Be a good bird*," then return it to the cage. A bird nipping during a step-up might be sensitively wobbled by the hand it is sitting on (see page 49). A bird being prompted to step-up might be distracted with a toy or other inanimate object when being given the prompt for "*Step-up*." We call this distraction technique "Good Hand/Bad Hand." It is described on page 55.

You might also choose to handle an otherwise well-adapted bird either with the towel or with hand-held perches during nippy stages. You might even discontinue interactive behavior for a while if you suspect that the bird is going through a wing feather molt, breeding season, or some other difficult transitional period. Don't give the bird any opportunity to bite. Careful techniques can help to maintain tameness here, for if the bird has no chance to bite, biting can't be reinforced.

## The Environment and Aggression

Raising or lowering the bird's usual relative height, combined with increasing access to rainfall, destruc-

tible chewables, and exercise will help to compensate for pent-up energy that might otherwise be expressed as aggression. A bird that suddenly becomes excessively territorial can benefit from having its cage moved or the cage interior redesigned.

Maturing greys occasionally decide that a particular chrome appliance is either a mate or a rival, leading to many courtships with toasters and wars with hair dryers. A grey parrot might decide that no one is allowed near the coffeepot. A bird that has fixated on a human-owned object must be denied access to that object. If it attacks a human-owned object, pick the bird up using a hand-held perch, a towel, or the "Good Hand/Bad Hand" technique, and replace the object with the approved surrogate enemy toy. Again, we must encourage and reward a companion grey for expressing hostility against the approved enemy toy. Hostile energy will be expressed somehow; it is best expressed against a toy.

As the bird matures, there will continue to be many times when it seeks human interaction. As we have discussed, patterning for cooperation with step-ups, the towel game, submissive interactions, and an ever-changing environment remain the most dependable ways to maintain companion behavior in a mature grey parrot.

## Chapter Four

# Selecting and Training a Talking Grey Parrot

**F**ascination with their legendary talking ability is the primary incentive that puts grey parrots into so many human homes. However, in the past, many companion grey parrots didn't acquire words until after one year of age.

*Greys may use vocal signals to indicate what they want.*

Today's premium baby greys are not only talking earlier, they are also speaking more openly. Even though greys have always enjoyed reputations as the best talking parrots, they were also known for being extremely quiet around strangers.

## Finding the Talking Baby

Male and female greys probably have equal ability to mimic, with both genders often acquiring large, constantly growing vocabularies. A more demonstrative, experimental, exuberant bird of either gender is more likely to want to communicate than a shy, withdrawn bird.

• Look for a bird that is interactive and interested in sights and sounds.

• Look for a baby that expresses interest and attention by leaning closer, stretching its wings—singly with a leg out or both shoulders stretched straight up—shaking the head while listening, or quickly wagging its tail from side to side. These easily observable happiness behav-

*A confident, well-socialized grey will eat a variety of foods.*

iors are indications that the bird is interested in what is going on around it.

• If the bird is old enough and has eyes that are light enough to see iris movement in contrast to the pupil of the eye, sometimes a grey will show interest by narrowing the pupils while keeping the eyelids almond-shaped. This is called "pinpointing" or "flashing."

A new owner may feel most confident about the bird's age, health, and socialization during hand-feeding by actually selecting a baby before it is weaned, and visiting frequently, usually once a week, to handle and interact with the bird. Speech training can begin before the bird is weaned, although, as we have repeatedly emphasized, grey parrots should be weaned by experienced professionals.

# Talking, Mimicking, and Signaling

## Talking and Mimicking

In the past, it was thought that one-on-one interaction, including much out-of-context repetition, was the best way to teach parrots to talk. If this works at all, these birds are more likely to merely mimic the sounds of the words rather than to use the words with associated meaning. Modern parrot fanciers are more excited about the prospect of talking rather than mimicking parrots, so our ways have changed.

The work of Dr. Irene Pepperberg demonstrated that attempts to train grey parrots with audio- and videotapes were useless.[1] Her bird, Alex, developed his abilities to speak with understanding through use of the model/rival method, in which one bird interacts with two humans who demonstrate the behaviors (words and identification) that are being trained. One trainer questions the other human about colors, shapes, and objects. This person is both modeling behavior and functioning as a rival for the trainer's attention. The model answers the question and receives a reward. Sometimes, roles of model/rival and trainer are reversed.

This technique probably resembles the way young parrots learn to communicate with their flock, by listening to older birds "duet" or talk back and forth.[2] Although it is best to include humans or other talking birds in this process, if the bird is young and not too distracted, or if the bird is properly conditioned, the

*Mealtime is a "flock" activity and a grey will expect to be included.*

"rival" might even be one of those stuffed, talking parrot plush toys or the family dog. Parrots often pick up names quickly due to the obvious response they get.

## Signaling

In addition to the acquisition of language, grey parrots, especially, acquire signaling behaviors. The most famous of the grey parrot's signals is probably that ear-splitting alarm call that is often used in captivity to demand attention. Grey parrots in the wild and in companion settings are fond of other types of signaling such as tapping the beak against the wall to mean: "Are you there?" "Is this hollow?" Or, they may make whistling or clicking sounds (happy recognition), or "gulping" interpretations of expressions of appreciation such as "*Oh, boy*" and "*Golly*."

Signals are less complex than actual language and may be more fun for birds. Some grey parrots enjoy signaling so much that they prefer signaling rather than language use. The most annoying signaling behaviors are often learned by companion greys for the purpose of getting immediate human attention. If a car alarm or smoke detector is annoying enough to make humans jump and to pay immediate frantic attention, then you can be sure that a young, gregarious grey parrot might learn to attract attention with that annoying signal after hearing it only once; in this case, the model/rival is the object making the noise.

# Setting the Stage for Talking

A baby parrot needs a tremendously stimulating environment. For at least the first two years, the baby grey's environment should look a little like a nursery school, with lots of toys and interesting things lying around. Repetition is important, but you should speak to the baby parrot just as you would speak to an infant, expecting it to learn the words it hears most often. Use words in context, just as you would use them with a baby. The bird doesn't have to be held during speech training; much of a young parrot's first communication efforts will probably be used to induce you to pick it up.

Try talking a little "baby (parrot) talk," for your first step to success might be in baby parrot language. If you can make a sound the bird is known to make, and the bird repeats the sound, It can then be rewarded with praise and affection, and you will have established the pattern by which the bird will acquire words. Grey parrots love to learn to use the expressions "*Good bird*!" and "*Oh Boy*!" to signal happiness. Use soothing, cooing sounds if the bird is shy.

While a young grey will not usually be immediately able to repeat a word, early signs of progress include the bird sitting around "muttering" or "babbling" quietly. Expect to see pinpointing eyes at these times (see page 163). The baby parrot will pick up the cadence of human language first, with understandable words and phrases following after practice.

Early phrases that are easily acquired include "What'cha doin'" and anything with "itty" sounds such as "*Pretty bird*" and "*Here, kitty, kitty, kitty*." Once you start combining words into phrases, mix them up, like "Pretty kitty" and "What's kitty doin'?"

The most important part of teaching a grey parrot to talk is answering the bird. The more the flock responds, even to "baby bird talk," the more the young bird will practice.

While grey parrots can easily copy words from humans of either gender, it's not unusual for African greys to acquire deep "male" voices. The voice the bird mimics can tell us which human the bird is most bonded to, for greys, especially, tend to mimic the voice of the perceived human rival for the affections of their favorite person.

Singing quietly, almost directly, into the grey parrot's head is an excellent way to get its undivided attention. Grey parrots, even talking ones, don't pinpoint or flash their eyes as much as Amazons or *Poicephalus*, so the absence of obvious eye movement is not necessarily an indication that a grey won't talk.

# Whistling Games and Daily Activities

Whistling games can be wonderful entertainment for both the bird and human flockmates. These games are probably virtually unavoidable with a grey parrot. Copying tunes from each other and adding onto the other's song can be a source of entertainment as well as bonding. Use whistling as fun and words for labeling actions and objects; however, if you run over to the bird when it whistles instead of encouraging it to say *"Come here"* or *"Step-up,"* the bird will lose the motivation to learn these words.

Be sure to include the young parrot in daily activities: eating, sleeping, showering, and expressing affection to other humans and animals. These activities replicate the feeling of being part of the flock and should stimulate the baby parrot's natural instinct to communicate with other flock members. If there is no problem with aggression, some grey parrots benefit from being allowed to sit higher than anybody else during speech training.

A baby grey will learn the most exciting words it hears are useful words that are spoken with the most gusto and enthusiasm, or words that get the biggest reaction. Therefore, profanity and angry words might be learned with only one repetition if the bird is really "tuned in" to humans in the household.

Some grey parrots talk first for attention, so they might try to talk more when they can hear, but not see humans. They talk first for attention in order to get out of the cage. This stimulus has been called "barrier frustration," for it has long been observed that caged birds or birds housed around a corner or screen appear to talk more than birds housed on open perches. This predisposition to vocalize in the presence of barriers is also a possible consequence of the feeling of safety provided by barriers. This doesn't mean that a grey will start talking if moved to another room. In some cases, you might want to spend time in another room to give the bird a chance to talk.

## The Guaranteed Talking Parrot

Sometimes, even though humans have done everything possible to encourage the bird to talk, it doesn't. Every bird is an individual, and not every individual wants to communicate with language. The only way to be absolutely guaranteed a talking grey parrot is to acquire a bird that is already talking. Sometimes this means looking for a young talking bird; sometimes it means acquiring a parrot that is mature. An exciting new home and an exciting new environment often brings new words and happy new behaviors into a mature bird's routines.

[1] Irene M. Pepperberg, Limited Contextual Vocal Learning in the Grey Parrot *(Psittacus erithacus):* The Effect of Interactive Co-Viewers on Videotaped Instruction. Lisa I. Gardiner, and Lori J. Luttrell; *Journal of Comparative Psychology*, 1999, Vol. 113, No. 2, pp. 158–172.
[2] Irene M. Pepperberg, Interview, December, 1995.

## Chapter Five

# General Care

## Environment: What Does a Grey Parrot Really Need?

**A** well-planned environment is the most direct way to a confident, well-behaved grey parrot. A safe cage in a secure location allows successful adjustment in these potentially sensitive birds, but safe physical components are only part of a well-planned environment. Many elements of the behavioral and social environment must be considered when seeking to maintain good behavior in a grey parrot.

## The Bird Cage

The best and the brightest parrot deserves the best equipment, and the cage is a very important part of that. Recent advances in cage design have brought us truly bird-proof latches and wonderful mess catchers that contain both the mess *and* the bird. Today's premium cages are often powder coated, occasionally stainless steel. Some of them have tear-off rolls of paper to simplify cage cleaning. Most of them are self-supporting units on wheels for easy access to cleaning, and many of them have three or more bowls for food and water.

The cage is the grey parrot's retreat. This is where the bird can relax and feel secure. No surprises occur here. There are toys to play with and food to eat. There are no demands made and no threats. The cage is a haven.

Left unsupervised, a grey parrot can roam. It might decide to chew on an electrical cord, eat a poisonous plant, or take a dive into the toilet (see Hazards in the Home on page 68). A bird cannot be counted on to make wise decisions while traversing the human world. A cage is necessary to provide the bird with physical as well as emotional security.

### The Baby Cage

A baby grey can easily have a bad reaction to the wrong first cage. The first cage should be small, safe, intimate. A baby grey might thrash, fall, nip, and demand attention in a cage that is too large. A very young bird might revert to wanting to be hand-fed. It might begin chewing feathers or developing fearful behaviors. These behaviors can indicate that the bird is feeling insecure.

Cages with few horizontal bars are difficult for a young bird that is still struggling with coordination to climb. Young birds will often seek security in small, close, places. A large cage might not provide the security a juvenile bird requires.

A good-sized first cage for a baby grey parrot is probably about 20 × 20 × 28 inches (51 × 51 × 71 cm) with ¾-inch (19 mm) spaces between the bars. A cage less than 18 inches (46 cm) deep can sometimes make a bird feel more exposed than protected because it cannot move back into the cage very far. To increase a shy bird's feeling of security, the top of the cage might be covered or partially covered with a gray towel extending down 4 or 5 inches (10 or 13 cm) on all sides of the cage. The bird can go up into the top for privacy in much the same way it might go up into a tree.

**Note:** Such a cage cover is best placed on the cage while the baby bird is not inside.

If you already own a large permanent cage for the new parrot, the bird's perception of the cage can be manipulated by raising the grate, making the cage seem smaller. Simply use self-locking cable ties, available in the electrical department of the hardware store, to secure the grate, or a homemade false grate to a higher group of horizontal bars. Once

the youngster begins developing confidence and independence, the grate can be lowered. If it's difficult or impossible to raise the grate, some birds benefit more from having low perches added near the bottom than having them gradually raised as coordination and confidence increase.

## The Permanent Cage

By the time a grey parrot is past a year old, it has usually developed the confidence necessary to be moved to a permanent cage. A cage used only for "roosting" or sleeping at night doesn't have to be large. However, if the bird is expected to spend much of the day in the cage while the family is at work, or if the bird has to stay in the cage for extended periods when its owners are on vacation, a larger cage is required. A cage about 2 feet deep, by 3 feet wide, by 4 feet high (61 × 91 × 122 cm), which makes the top 5 feet (152 cm) from the floor if the cage legs are a foot (30 cm) tall, is probably best. This is enough space for a grey parrot, Red-tail or Timneh, to feel happy and secure.

Each bird's emotional needs are also a factor in determining proper cage size. Some grey parrots do not feel secure in a cage that is too large. A small percentage of greys seem almost claustrophobic in a cage that is too small. A cage that seems appropriate to one grey parrot might cause neurotic behaviors in another.

Usability of the cage is another factor in determining proper size. Cages with horizontal side bars encourage these very agile climbers to get their exercise by climbing up and down the sides. While they can certainly climb up and down vertical cage bars if they really want to, they must have more motivation to do so. Without horizontal bars, they will climb up and down less often and rely on walking back and forth on the perches for entertainment. At least two sides of the cage—on the sides or the front and back—should have all horizontal bars. A cage with too few horizontal bars will contribute to sedentary behavior and lack of curiosity. Avoid round or cylindrical cages, as shy grey parrots find safety in cage corners.

## Cage Features

A large door helps to prevent fearful behaviors involving going in and out of the cage. The bird should be able to sit comfortably on the hand without having to duck while going through the door, as passing through openings of any kind can be problematic for many birds. Having a large enough cage door can help prevent some individuals from being reluctant to go into or out of the cage on the hand; step-up practice can add to the bird's comfort in performing this procedure.

In selecting the optimum cage, consider the following:
• The composition or material the cage is made of
• The structure or design of the cage
• The quality of the cage
• The suitability of perches and other accessories

*This cage provides horizontal bars for easy climbing, a large door, and enough room for interesting toys.*

• The ease with which the cage can be serviced

**Material:** A parrot cage is best made from noncorrosive metal. Acceptable substances include steel, brass, or chrome, and welded wire that is no longer shiny. Powder-coated cages will usually stand up to the test of the grey parrot's beak and are usually very safe. A wooden cage will eventually be reduced to toothpicks, no matter what kind of wood is used. Hardware cloth or shiny welded wire have zinc, which is toxic, in the coating.

Welded wire can be made safe by scrubbing the surfaces with detergent or vinegar and a wire brush, or by leaving the cage outside and exposed to the elements until it becomes dull. Hardware cloth is always dangerous to chewing birds. The grey parrot's strong beak can easily remove and possibly swallow paint from the bars of a painted cage.

**Bars:** The cage should be structured so that there are no openings and spaces between the bars large enough for the bird to put its head through or small enough to catch a toe. Ornamental wires or bars should usually be avoided. Many birds will get legs or feet caught in bars that form a V, such as where the bars come together in a domed-top cage. Round cages tend to promote fearfulness. A grey parrot feels much more secure if the flat backside of the cage is against a wall. Many grey parrots demonstrate an obvious preference for corners.

A good-quality cage will have bars that are too thick for the bird to bend. The places where the bars join will be smooth. There will be no sharp edges within the parrot's reach and it will not be easy to disassemble, or the bird will take it apart. The finish cannot be flaky. Remember that the bird might live in this cage for 40 years or more.

**Perches:** Perches that come in the cage may or may not be suitable for either a Red-tailed or Timneh grey parrot. Many larger cages come with hardwood perches that are size-appropriate for much larger birds such as cockatoos and macaws. These perches are often too large for a grey to grip, and as you are probably well aware by now, the grey parrot loves to grip the perch and flap.

Both hand-held and stationary perches should be provided in a variety of easily gripped sizes. For the bird to be able to grip the perch, the opposing long toes need to extend at least a little more than halfway around. Soft wood branches, such as those of any of the poplar family, are suitable perching surfaces as long as much of the bark is intact. Fruit trees such as plum and citrus are also excellent perch material. Avoid materials that are too hard, too smooth, or too rough. Types of perches that are not suitable include manzanita, dowel rods, "grooming" perches, and plastic or PVC perches.

A grey parrot's feet were designed to stand on branches with bark on them. The skin on the bottom of the feet needs the texture of the bark to stay in good condition. Poor perches will cause soft or worn spots to form on the bottoms of the feet. These spots can become sores and cause serious problems for the bird. Branches from trees are less expensive and healthier for the bird. Remember to cut several so that there are spares and to scrub them with soap and water and leave them in the sun to dry.

**Note:** African grey parrots love to spend lots of time on top of their cages holding on and flapping like crazy. The cage top should easily accommodate this activity. If a cage-top perch is used, be sure that the highest point where the bird can sit comfortably is also easily gripped for strenuous flapping.

**Trays and Grates:** The cage should also be easy to clean, with a removable tray and, preferably, a removable grate. Grey parrots like to play on the bottom of the cage and a grate will keep them from playing in their droppings and any old food that can be a disease risk. The bars of the grate should be as close together as the bars in the rest of the cage.

**Dishes:** If the cage you like comes with aluminum dishes, replace them. Stainless steel or ceramic bowls are easier to keep clean and will last longer.

## Introducing a Grey Parrot to a New Cage

It's not unusual for an African grey parrot to have an adverse reaction to a new cage or to the way it is introduced into a new cage, especially if a bird has been in only one cage, such as a baby cage, its entire life, or if it has been in the same cage for many years.

While some greys can merely be removed from one cage and locked into another cage, most are best induced to choose to move to a new cage. This is accomplished by placing the new cage in the position of

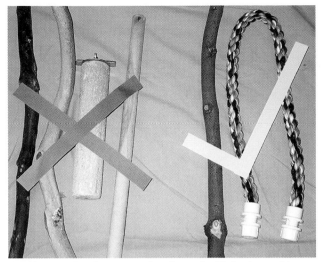

*Perches made of rope or natural wood with bark provide the best surfaces for a grey's feet.*

the beloved old cage with the old cage beside it. If the bird freely enters the new cage and seeks toys and food there, food and water can be removed from the old cage during the day. By the third or fourth day, if the bird is eating in the new cage, the old cage can have all toys and perches removed and can be set on the floor so that the bird will more or less have to "choose" the new cage.

## Cage Location

Feelings of happiness, safety, and security should be associated with the location of the cage. A grey parrot likes to be in an area where it can experience the most interaction with its human flock members and still feel safe. Many greys live in dining rooms and living rooms, but a cage that is exposed on all sides will not

## Hazards in the Home

African greys are sometimes injured or killed in household accidents. The majority of these accidents are associated with access to:

• Standing water—bathtub, toilet, sink, hot tub, aquarium
• Frying pans, cooking stoves, and open fireplaces
• Entanglement trauma: loose strings in toys, towels, and afghans
• Open doors and windows
• Larger pets
• Ceiling fans, electrical cords, swinging doors, recliners
• Inappropriate bar spacing or poorly designed caging
• Toxic plants
• Toxic fumes from second-hand smoke
• Almost any burning plastic, including polytetrafluroethelyene (Teflon)
• Unsupervised access to unsafe toys
• Household pesticides, human medications, room deodorants
• Dietary toxins including alcohol, avocado, chocolate, moldy foods

seem secure, so avoid placing the cage in the middle of the room or against a window.

An "ideal" location to most African grey parrots would typically be as high as the bird's disposition allows, against a wall, and across the room from entrances and heavy traffic areas. A bird located beside a high-traffic doorway could experience fear reactions whenever anyone rushed unexpectedly through. Shelter may be important to a grey parrots' feelings of safety, and greys just love peeking out from behind plants and toys, but height is probably the most significant factor in stimulating feelings of safety in most African grey parrots. If there is a tendency for a particular grey parrot to be shy or fearful, that tendency can sometimes be improved by changing height.

## The Roost Cage

Many grey parrots and their households find great benefit from having a separate cage for the bird to sleep in—a roost cage. This roost cage need not be large or fancy, for it is merely a quiet place to sleep away from the hustle and bustle of human evening activities. Ten to twelve hours of sleep per night are recommended for the grey, and a roost cage can help fill this need for a quiet place to sleep. The baby cage that the bird came home in is probably perfect for this purpose. This familiar second cage is also good for vacations and other longer outings.

# The Home Environment

## Height and Attitude

Height manipulations can stimulate changes in a parrot's attitude. A grey parrot may be noticeably sensitive to height, which can stimulate feelings either of territorial aggression, in a bold bird, or safety, in a shy bird. Shy greys might find more security in being housed low, while outgoing birds would not tolerate it. A dominant bird will defend a position of control whether it is the door of the cage, a food dish, or someone's back.

If the bird is learning to bite, make changes to prevent the reinforcement of biting into a pattern by removing the bird's control using a perch to pick it up through the door of the cage, not allowing shoulder access, and removing or replacing food dishes only when the bird is in another place. Lower birds that are demonstrating territorial or manipulation biting; raise or lower the position of fear biters, depending upon their responses (see Common Causes of Biting, page 109).

Although we begin with an assumption that height may be causing territorial aggression, trial-and-error changes might demonstrate that the reverse is true. Aggression may be difficult to distinguish from fear because of the grey parrots' well-developed fight-or-flight response, especially the first part of the fight-or-flight response— fear biting. Either raising or lowering the height of a nipping bird might bring a feeling of safety and eliminate the need to nip. Additionally, a shy bird may experience enhanced confidence by merely having the height of the cage raised or the perches that are customarily used.

## On the Shoulder

Allowing a grey parrot on the shoulder can easily contribute to displaced or overt aggression in a territorial bird or in one that manipulates with aggression. A human might be bitten trying to remove a grey parrot from the shoulder, but height is not the only factor that influences aggression on the shoulder; some of it has to do with the inability to make eye contact when the bird is there. Any bird with a well-patterned step-up response will usually step-up with eye contact. Without eye contact, the pattern is not being repeated and the bird may feel dominant and choose not to cooperate with the step-up. Although it is probably less dangerous to humans to allow a grey parrot on the shoulder than other larger hookbills, we do not

*A grey parrot on the shoulder may bite out of fear or territorialism.*

recommend it except in situations where a frightened bird may need the extra security.

Additionally, allowing a grey parrot on the shoulder is potentially dangerous to the bird. The floor can be a long fall, and grey parrots occasionally incur split breast injuries in such falls. Fear of falling can also be harmful to the bird.

## Change

An African grey parrot can become excessively concerned with control of its cage territory. This tendency to avoid anything unfamiliar is probably slightly greater in the Red-tailed greys than in Timnehs.

A grey parrot's environment should be regularly, sensitively altered. This is an important part of early socialization. Grey parrots must be taught as neonates and juveniles to tolerate and enjoy change. They are especially receptive to manipulation of environmental elements as a means of controlling both aggression and fearfulness by increasing tolerance to change.

Actually, lack of planned, appropriate changes can damage a grey parrot's personality. If a companion grey parrot is not provided with interesting, reasonable changes, ill effects on behavior may be evident by the time the bird is one year old. We can reduce aggression and enhance the bird's sense of safety during changes by conditioning the bird to tolerate having its cage and play areas moved at least a couple of times yearly. This could mean merely reversing the position of the cage and the play area, or it could mean using other locations in the home.

Some grey parrots are extremely intolerant of human intervention in the arrangement of toys or perches. These birds' toys or perches should be rearranged only when the bird is out of sight of the cage. Rearranging perches can also bring behavioral benefits. Occasional introduction—at least three times a year—of new and differently configured branches will provide interesting new perspectives for a happy, confident, nonaggressive bird.

## Enriching the Environment

The grey parrots' ancestors evolved a metabolism that was equipped to cope with a life of wild independence. A companion parrot's indoor environment is often missing important elements such as flying, foraging, and nest site preparation that the bird would experience in the wild. These activities enable the bird to express energy that results naturally from its metabolism. When energy is unused, as in a wing feather-trimmed companion bird sitting in a cage ("couch potato"), that energy is frequently expressed as inappropriate behaviors. Unexpressed nervous energy can appear as fearfulness, screeching, or feather-damaging behaviors (see Feathers and Feather Problems, page 128).

In the wild, the bird would be physically and intellectually stimulated by elements of the environment related to survival. The wild

*Some greys enjoy their flapping exercises so much that they will do them on command.*

African parrot spends most of its time foraging for food. In captivity that food is provided for it in a bowl. We must find ways for the bird to use the energy that would be used during foraging in the wild.

## Exercise

It is impossible for a captive bird to get as much exercise as it would get in the wild. Young greys are quick to start practicing and getting into shape for the flying they anticipate. They will stand on the door of the cage or perch where they can flap unfettered. They will, on their own, flap until they are out of breath. Many greys, shortly after fledging, will discontinue this type of exercise

voluntarily and need to be encouraged to continue. Greys that haven't done it in years may have to be reminded of the benefits.

Exercise helps relieve stress and boredom in birds just as it does in humans. It improves circulation and the flow of oxygen throughout the body. Much of a grey's self-confidence comes from knowing its wings will "work" and feeling the resistance of the air against wing feathers.

Check the state of the wing feathers before expecting the grey to want to flap. Many greys that are actively growing in feathers are very protective of them and will refuse to risk breaking them by flapping.

Some greys will even want to stay in their cages to make sure they won't have to flap. A grey with actively growing primary feathers should not be asked to flap against its will.

You can encourage a young grey to exercise by slowly rotating the hand it is perched on. The bird will flap to maintain balance. Many older greys will give up on flapping and just hold on tighter to the hand. Moving your hand up and down while holding onto the toes can be a little stronger encouragement. For greys that are having a hard time getting an exercise program started, you can try holding the bird about

### Toy Trick

If a grey parrot is afraid of new toys, perches, or other objects in the environment, we can try to manipulate the bird's perception of these elements by having each new thing wear the same "disguise" as all the other things.

That is, if a paper towel or square pop-up tissue is rolled diagonally and tied around each toy like a cowpoke's bandanna, then the bird will be interested in removing the paper towel "bows" in order to play with the toys. If each new toy comes with a paper towel or tissue bow, then no toy is ever viewed as a new toy; every toy looks much like the last toy, and they all have that first part (the bow) that has to be removed to get to the fun stuff. The bird will never fear a new toy again.

2 or 3 feet (61 to 91 cm) over a bed and causing the bird to fall off the hand or arm and onto the soft mattress. Once the parrot gets the idea, it will start to enjoy the exercise and will look forward to doing it regularly.

It is almost impossible to provide a grey as much exercise as it is designed to handle. Allowing the bird to flap until it is breathing hard should be done at least once a day.

## Decision Making

Another part of foraging involves decision-making processes. Parrots develop more stable emotions and more confident dispositions from having access to appropriate choices— when more than one of a particular element such as food, toys, and/or perches are provided simultaneously. Since all the toys and perches are appropriate, no matter which one the bird chooses, the decision will be a successful decision and the bird will have a happy, self-rewarding interaction with its environment. Even if the bird chooses not to try one of the new foods, toys, or perches, these elements have given the bird opportunities to experience confidence as a result of making a successful decision between alternatives.

## Toys and Other Accessories

Grey parrots need destructible toys and perches. Those strong, sharp beaks are there for a purpose, and if destructible chewables are not provided, the bird will find them. Paper, leather, wood, branches, bark, cork, cardboard, cloth, and rope—or whatever the bird decides is necessary—must be provided on a regular basis. Destructible accessories should be replaced and rotated as often as required by the bird. Owners easily fall into the trap of getting a toy that is chewed up in a few days and replacing it with a toy that can't be chewed up so easily. However, the reason the bird chewed up the toy so fast is because it has a need to do so, and giving it a toy it can't chew up is denying it the chance to fill a need (see Battling Boredom, page 75).

## Rainfall and Bathing

Wild grey parrots spent thousands of years, hundreds of generations, evolving a metabolism that would enable them to function fully in the rain. That means that grey parrots can forage for food, nest, reproduce, feed, and raise young while they are wet. Rainfall is missing in the companion setting, and all the energy birds need to survive wet is unused. This lost access to rainfall represents lost exercise.

Some of the lost opportunities to express energy and to burn calories and frustration can be replaced by treating the bird to frequent drenching showers. The energy expressed by bathing and recovering from being wet helps to prevent some of those temper tantrums that can occur so frequently in captivity.

Grey parrots are famously reluctant to enjoy showers, although this

*Toys that are easy to chew or destroy are essential to meeting the parrot's needs.*

can be easily learned from baby Amazons. Companion grey parrots are more likely to enjoy bathing in a bowl; sometimes just a shallow bowl of water is enough. While this is better than not bathing at all, it has some disadvantages:

**1.** The bird's back doesn't get wet, and those feathers can remain soiled.

**2.** Since the bird really doesn't get wet, it doesn't use the requisite amount of energy usually expended by a parrot that flies around in rainfall, then later recovers from being wet.

**3.** It fouls both the water and the bird.

Showers can supplement and replace some of the bird's own bathing efforts (see page 73). Sometimes, a quick shower just as fresh water is provided in the bowl will stimulate an immediate bath, and water can be replaced at the end of the servicing cycle.

Although companion grey parrots do sometimes enjoy sharing showers with their humans, regular showerheads are usually too harsh and forceful for most greys to enjoy. Some African greys also resist a spray-bottle shower. A particular bird may have to be conditioned to enjoy being sprayed. Hold the bottle, faucet-connected spraying device, or pump-up sprayer lower than the bird and spray a continuous mist over the bird's head so that the water falls down on the bird like rainfall. If the bird is reluctant to accept a shower, discontinuing eye contact when spraying may help. Sometimes demonstrating (modeling) enjoyment of the shower, possibly with another person or bird, can stimulate a grey parrot to accept the shower. If the bird is to be thoroughly wet, it's best to bathe in the morning so that there's ample time for the bird to dry naturally before nightfall.

Here are some hints for stimulating an enjoyable shower time:
• Spray the bird while it is dipping its head into the water dish to take a bath.
• Change the water temperature (warmer or cooler).
• Increase the room temperature.
• Run the vacuum cleaner or other artificial waterfall sounds.
• Prime the bird for the shower by spraying a little, then coming back a minute later and spraying more.

*Hearing the sound of running water can get a reluctant grey in the mood for a shower.*

• Change the location where the shower is offered—on the cage, in the cage, in a playpen, and so on.
• Change the time of day (earlier or later).
• Change the type of spray (smaller or larger drops) or appearance (color) of spray bottle.

# Battling Boredom

A bird in the wild never experiences boredom; a wild bird in a captive environment does not naturally know how to overcome it. When a parrot is completely dependent upon humans or one human for all its intellectual, emotional, and physical stimulation, it fails to develop independent play habits and curiosity. Grey parrots are notorious for alleviating boredom in ways that are either self-destructive or detrimental to the bird/human relationship.

### What Is a Toy?

A toy is a tool for the provision of self-rewarding behavior. It is designed to be enjoyable to use, even though it has no purpose other than the process of using it.

Humans are very comfortable with the idea of giving toys to children and animals. Most of the recipients are happy to see the toys and know immediately what to do with them. However, many greys suffer from boredom in a cage filled with toys.

You'd think a creature as smart as a parrot should be able to figure out what to do with a toy, but the grey's intelligence depends upon its ability to learn new things and to apply already known concepts to new situations. For greys, curiosity and playfulness must be demonstrated by human caregivers or by other birds.

### The Grey Parrot That Played Like an Amazon

Almost all my baby Amazons play a game with each other that might be called Chicken: Two birds hang upside down by one foot, locking the other foot with their opponent's foot and then wrestling until one or both fall.

Belana is a Red-tailed grey that was raised with a Double Yellow-headed Amazon. Belana's cagemate was particularly fond of this Chicken game and insisted that Belana learn it. The grey parrot learned to be very good at the game and often won.

Eventually, Belana shared a cage with an older Red-tailed grey. She was very excited to have another cagemate and immediately went to the top of the cage to initiate a game of Chicken. The other grey was horrified and let her know it! Subsequently, Belana began to copy behavior from this older grey and dropped the game from her repertoire. She was never able to teach the Chicken game to him, but he did learn other games from her, including tug-of-war and the thrills of shredding wood.

*Simply providing many toys may not be enough to stimulate a grey to play.*

Baby greys learn a great deal from their "clutchmates." When two or three juvenile greys are confronted with a foreign object, if the clutch leader is afraid of it, the others will assume it is a scary thing and will copy the behavior of the first bird. A grey that is raised with an Amazon— typically a more brazen, fearless bird—might be less likely to give in to its instinctual fight-or-flight response. A grey parrot that is raised with an Amazon will, more likely, learn to shred or beat up an object in the manner demonstrated (modeled) by the Amazon. This goes for interactive games as well.

The act of releasing pent-up natural behaviors on toys provides physical and emotional release and enhances the development of curiosity. The reduction of stress is an incentive to continue engaging in these activities. This is common self-rewarding behavior. The more often the bird finds new things that can be used in this way, the more it will be compelled to find new things that can also be used in this way, and the bird will begin investigating objects to determine which ones can be used as toys.

Greys learn best by example. There is no better way to get a grey interested in something than to let it see that someone else is so interested in it that it isn't shared. When introducing a toy to an African grey, pretend the bird isn't allowed to have it. Show it to the grey, but take it away before the bird has a chance to show that it's afraid of it. The "teacher" should be really excited about the toy. Show the toy to the bird briefly again, then give the toy to someone else who acts excited over it. Show it to the bird again. Give it to another bird, or to the dog, or to a child, while frequently showing it to the bird and taking it away again.

The grey parrot will start to lean toward the toy instead of away from it. At some point it will tentatively touch it. Whisk it away again. When the grey becomes more insistent and you think it will actually hold onto it, you can give the toy to the bird with much praise for agreeing to explore the new object. This works with food as well.

At some point, the African grey *must* learn to play with toys. For many greys this is a gradual process that starts when they are old enough to begin interacting with the other baby birds where they are being raised. There are greys, however, who do not have the luxury of learning from other parrots as they would in the wild and these birds must be taught by humans how to be birds. Human caregivers love to cuddle babies; baby greys love to cuddle. They are almost like baby cockatoos that will lie in a person's lap and be constantly hugged and petted. While affection is important to a grey parrot, these types of interactions will not help the bird learn to function for itself later.

To teach a grey to play with toys, humans must set an example when possible. Ripping paper, ringing bells dragging pieces of rope around while the parrot is watching from a distance can stimulate the bird to copy these behaviors. For greys that will still sit on a lap, placing toys in the lap and gently pawing at them and playing with them will help get the bird interested.

The handler might attach toys to a shirt where the bird will be likely to pick at them in the way it might pick at a button or jewelry. Spreading toys out on the floor and demonstrating playing can encourage curiosity. An older grey might prefer to watch this display from a perch,

while a younger one may be more inclined to join in. If the bird perceives the human to be a respected and important flock member, it will learn while watching.

Some greys grab and rip paper if the paper is in the way. Once they discover that this is fun, they begin ripping more things. Placing paper pompoms in the cage next to a favorite perch or hanging down where they are in the way can stimulate the bird to experiment with these paper objects and, subsequently, toys. Watch carefully, especially with Timnehs, to ensure that the bird isn't actually eating the paper.

The following toys can be used to encourage playing:
• A piece of cheap box tape (the kind that isn't too sticky) wrapped around a chunk of cotton rope not more than 1.5 inches (3.8 cm) long, or around a strip of denim cut on the bias like shoestring tips.
• Paper egg cartons laid on top of the cage so the bird has to chew them through the bars.
• Wooden spoons.
• Pompoms made from newspaper or other plain, not shiny, paper.
• Cardboard tubes.
• Whole rolls of untreated, clean, unused bathroom tissue that has not been stored in the bathroom.
• Dull paper junk mail on a skewer made for birds or woven in the cage bars.
• Old jeans or cotton material cut into strips, on the bias so the strings aren't long, and tied to the cage bars or to other toys.

- Popsicle sticks.
- Paper cups or paper plates. Holes can be punched in them and straws woven through. Remember: Any rope or string given to the bird should be short enough to not accidentally wrap around the neck or feet.
- Plastic straws.
- Some plastic toys made for children; make sure the bird's toes and feet can't get caught in them.
- A toothbrush. Be careful because some toothbrushes have bristles that are anchored with tiny pieces of metal, often toxic. You can see the pieces if the toothbrush is one of the clear type.
- Favorite end tables, the arms of the chairs, and prized pieces of heirloom furniture (well, grey parrots *think* those make great toys!).

It's not unusual for humans to be proud of the fact that they don't have to worry about getting new toys all the time because their grey never chews things up. This should be considered a behavior problem to be addressed with corrective measures. While that particular bird may not have developed any problems the owner finds annoying, it cannot live for 50 years without entertaining itself in some way. If this is not done by chewing and playing with toys, it will probably be accomplished with screaming or feather mutilation.

## Vocalization Games

A typical African grey enjoys the art of vocal communication. Greys want to join in the conversations going on among other flock members. A companion grey picks up the cadence of conversations and begins interjecting words and phrases such as "*Uh huh*," "*Okay*," "*That's right*," in addition to well-timed chuckles.

Simply by talking to an African grey while performing daily rituals

### Listening to Your Grey Parrot

My Red-tailed African grey, Bob, came to me as a feather plucker. His previous owner showered him with attention and toys and, despite diligent efforts, could not convince him to stop damaging feathers. When he was nine years old, she gave him to me.

Almost immediately, I began to use word labels for as many things as possible when interacting with him. He learned the words "*Step-up*," "*head scratch*," "*want some*," "*shower*," and "*breakfast*," among other things.

One day I was engrossed in some housework and was paying little attention to Bob. (It can be entirely too easy to ignore them when they are being good and not being obnoxious.) I realized he was talking but I was not listening to the words. Suddenly there was a loud hacking cough, like someone with pneumonia. Startled, I looked over at Bob. He tilted his head and said "*Oh Bob! Head scratch!*"

I taught him the words; he decided he needed to teach me to listen to them.

and labeling things that are part of the parrot's daily life, the bird will pick up language that will help it join in the flock's activities. The parrot benefits on many levels from this interaction. It learns to trust the owner who always lets it know what will happen next, it learns to ask for the things it needs and so gains self-confidence by being in control of certain aspects of life, and it feels loyalty to the flock because of being able to vocally join in.

Greys love to whistle. A human who lives with a grey can have great whistling contests with the bird. A grey parrot is capable of learning a whole song, but may prefer to do solos in the middle or join one song with another, or take pieces from many songs and piece them together. They are almost always grateful for input from their human companions. These jam sessions can go on and on, finally leaving humans doubled over in laughter.

## Changes of Scenery

As previously mentioned, changes of scenery are important in reducing boredom and promoting curiosity. A grey parrot can experience a change of scenery simply by being moved from one room to another. If a particular bird gets nervous in another room or is unaccustomed to experiencing new surroundings, changes must be made gradually. The person in whom the bird has the most confidence should be the one to show the new room to the parrot. If the

*A basket can be easily made into a portable perch, making it easy to give the bird a change of scenery.*

bird becomes anxious or fearful, don't force it to stay in the new room. The bird will gradually allow longer visits to new places, unless it feels it can't escape. In that case a panic reaction can set in, so it's best to try to read the bird's mood and retreat before the bird gets too upset. Sometimes allowing the bird to visit the new place while enclosed in the safety of a familiar, comfortable carrier will help the bird bypass the feelings of insecurity it might have outside the carrier.

Chances are, most parrots will not live out their lives in one household. Most people do not live in the same house for 50 or 60 years. If a parrot is allowed to develop a very narrow sense of secure places, it could find it devastating when a move is necessary. A bird that is carefully introduced to unfamiliar places will become more open to going to other new places and will be much better off when inevitable changes occur.

# Diet

Diet is the first step in preventing and solving all health and behavior problems. Feeding an African grey can be like trying to feed a spoiled child; they can be "picky eaters." However, most greys are naturally very food-focused and will eat almost anything. Sometimes, finicky eating becomes a game, a game of who trains whom.

Many parrots remain on poor diets because some owners mistakenly believe that since there have been no health problems, the diet must be okay. However, because greys are naturally healthy-looking birds, they may appear fit while, in reality, they are suffering from nutritional imbalances. By the time they succumb to disease, they may have very few resources left that would allow them to heal. So when a bird has been on a sunflower seed and french fry diet for the last ten years, and "it isn't dead yet!" this doesn't mean the bird won't be deathly ill tomorrow.

While nearly everyone who feeds parrots has a notion of what to feed, how much to feed, and when to feed it, today's bird owner can take advantage of tremendous advances in the science of avian nutrition. Both the basic nutritional needs of the bird—what vitamins the parrot needs and what foods contain those vitamins—and the general eating habits of parrots—how to promote good habits and discourage bad ones—are important. Consider the following factors when planning a parrot's diet:

• In general, a parrot's nutritional needs are not much different from human nutritional needs.

• Vitamins obtained through food sources are more useful and less dangerous than chemically added vitamins.

• The best way to supply a variety of nutrients is to supply a variety of foods.

• A grey will not automatically eat nutritious food. Instead, when offered a large amount of food, it will select what it likes best.

• Some birds, when consistently offered a large amount of food, will eat for recreation and not develop more healthy ways of entertaining themselves.

• Parrots often resist change.

• Good habits are easiest to establish at an early age.

• Parrots will use the "flock" around them as a role model for what to eat.

• Excess fat, preservatives, and artificial ingredients are not good for birds.

Many of these points may seem familiar since most also apply to humans and other warm-blooded animals. Unfortunately, getting proper nutrition into a grey is not as simple as mixing the proper proportions of ingredients and putting them into a dish. You must also ensure that the nutrients are actually getting into the bird in the proper proportions.

## Nutrients

Avian nutrition deserves volumes on its own, and parrot owners should consider investing in a book on this subject. Barron's handy *Feeding Your Pet Bird* by Petra Burgmann, D.V.M., is a useful resource. As an overview, the following tips should be helpful in devising a suitable diet for your grey.

**Vegetables:** Vegetables are the best source of vitamins and minerals. They can be served fresh, thawed, raw, or lightly cooked. If one-third to one-half of a grey parrot's diet consists of carefully selected vegetables, many of the requirements for vitamins and minerals will be met. Some vegetables contain many more nutrients than others. Sweet potatoes, carrots, yellow squash, collard or dandelion greens, kale and broccoli (sources of calcium), chard, beets and beet tops, and peppers (green or hot) are especially good sources of vitamins A, K, and E. Other good vegetable choices include peas, green beans, leaf (rather than head) lettuce, lima beans, navy beans (also good for calcium), various types of sprouts, celery, zucchini, and cucumbers.

## Toby's Seed

Robin's eight-year-old Red-tailed grey, Toby, went to work with her every day. Toby was a very spoiled constant companion. When the bird came down with a salmonella infection due to a weakened immune system, it became apparent that his diet needed improvement.

I was baby-sitting Toby shortly after his recovery and took the opportunity to see if he would eat a healthier diet, including pellets instead of seed. He did not hesitate to eat whatever I put in front of him. Robin was stunned at the progress when she came to pick him up. She very gladly acquired a premium manufactured diet for her bird.

I talked with Robin a few weeks later and learned that Toby was back on a seed diet. Robin said she couldn't get him to eat anything else. It seems that when Robin put any other food in front of him, Toby would throw it and say "*Seed!*"

Robin tried to ignore him, but Toby would begin screeching and yelling "*Seed!*" "*Seed!*" until Robin relented and gave him seed.

Toby had not tried that with me, evidently realizing that I had not been properly "trained." Robin found it very difficult to get untrained, but her persistence eventually paid off, and Toby has been happily, healthily gobbling pellets and vegetables ever since.

**Note:** Corn does *not* appear on this list. Corn is not a good source of vitamins or minerals, but is a good source of calories. Any parrot can easily fill up on corn and avoid eating more nutritious selections.

**Pellets:** Another one-third to one-half of the diet can be comprised of high-quality pellets designed for companion parrots. Extensive research has gone into developing diets that will deliver balanced nutrition in every bite. Since the birds cannot remove some of the nutrients from the chunks and eat others, the pellet can help fill in the nutritional gaps. Pellets also make it easier to maintain balanced nutrition of the bird's diet on those days when you are in a hurry and cannot prepare a normal meal. It is also nice to be able to let the pet-sitter feed pellets for a few days when you're on vacation, rather than trying to teach a novice how to chop the proper balance of vegetables.

While there are many brands of pellets on the market, they are not all equal. Some have artificial colors and flavors, which, in a few instances, appear to have contributed to feather plucking. Some provide nutrition only through chemical additives, which are not always easily utilized by the body. Some appear to contain proper amounts of protein, but the protein may not be digestible or may not contain the proper variety of amino acids. Some have more natural ingredients, then taint them with preservatives. Some just taste bad. You should probably

*Good food choices include carrots, sweet potatoes, mango, papaya, squash, cantaloupe, beans, rice, and pasta.*

be willing to taste your birds' food. If *you* wouldn't eat it, the bird probably won't eat it either.

Assessing the quality of the pellet is easiest by reading the label. Much of the nutrition should be derived through food sources, such as grains, some seed, alfalfa, kelp, and spirulina. Organic food sources are preferable. Brands in which there are only two or three food sources and a long list of chemical additives should be avoided.

**Supplementing:** Although many pelleted diets claim to be the only food the bird needs, there are behavioral and nutritional advantages in supplementing with fresh natural foods as described here. The best way to get a variety of nutrients into a grey parrot is by offering a variety of foods in addition to pellets.

One popular way to convince the bird to eat a variety of foods is to incorporate healthy food choices into the human diet and share these with the bird. These food choices must be made carefully. Offer fruits such as papayas, mangos, cantaloupe, pomegranates, apples, and bananas. Almonds as well as some other tree nuts (not peanuts) have calcium. Corn bread, pasta, spaghetti (with sauce), pizza, small amounts of Swiss cheese or yogurt, cooked potatoes or rice, well-cooked chicken on the bone, soup (not hot!), chili, stir-fry, cereal, as well as many other foods, make good selections, presuming they are low in salt and fat. A parrot usually wants to eat whatever it sees its owner eat-

ing. Many people eat a healthier diet because they own a bird.

Sometimes a bird will gorge on such less than nutritious "extras" as pizza or corn. Use the bird's head as a judge of proportion. If the bird is being offered a portion that is the size of its head, ask yourself if you would eat a human head-sized portion of that food—or half that. Table foods should probably comprise less than 20 percent of a bird's diet.

A cooked mixture of soaked then cooked dry beans and grains is an easy-to-use source of different proteins. A large batch can be prepared and divided into portion sizes for freezing. Adding chopped sweet potatoes and other vegetables to the mix increases the vitamin content.

## Healthy Habits

If it could, an African grey might spend its whole day sifting through its food dish and rechewing the vegetables it already ate. Most babies start out doing this. A weaning African grey baby should have many food choices available most of the time, but once the bird is weaned and maintaining its weight with solid foods, it's time to work on healthy eating habits.

**Eating times:** Parrots typically have two primary eating times and, as long as they are healthy, do not require food available at all times. Morning is the biggest mealtime of the day. This is often the best time to offer vegetables and soft foods such as cooked grains. Pellets and small amounts of table food can be

## Mealworms

I'd come across accounts of parrot breeders offering "live food" such as mealworms during breeding season. Since I had some giant mealworms to feed my turtles, I thought I'd see what the birds would do with them. Placing a few worms into some of the food dishes, it was easy to see that the birds were horrified!

I removed the worms and proceeded to feed the turtles on the floor in front of the parrots. The turtles chased the worms and fought over them, gulping them down like kids with chocolate chip cookies.

The parrots watched intently and it wasn't long before my Red-tailed grey was saying: "*Want some!*"

I looked up and all of the birds were doing the tricks they do to get a treat. I handed one of them a mealworm and the others rushed over to try to take it away. It was my turn to be upset when I watched them eat the squirmy things. I would never have guessed that companion parrots would use turtles as role models!

offered in the evening. Grey parrots should not be fed so much at each meal that they cannot finish it.

Many parrot owners want to be kind to their birds by leaving food available for them at all times. They are worried that the bird might become hungry; however, being hungry is not really a bad thing. In the wild, hunger would motivate the birds to go find their next meal. Leaving food available at all times encourages bad habits such as picky eating and not playing with toys because they are playing with food instead and, if soft food is left in the cage, it may be spoiled when the bird goes to chew on it later. A grey that is fed smaller amounts will not eat its favorites and throw the rest to the ground. Many birds finish their morning meal within a few hours. This doesn't mean that the dish must be refilled. Most birds would probably choose to eat again in midafternoon, maybe around 3:00 or 4:00 P.M. They can learn to wait a few hours later if necessary. If you will be coming home very late, a small amount of dry pellets, which won't spoil, can be left in the cage. This should be discontinued if the bird becomes reluctant to eat the variety of food offered.

Mealtime is a social time for greys as for many other types of parrots. The bird will expect to eat at the same time as you and will want to be able to see the rest of the "flock" eating. Often, a good way to get a grey to eat new foods is to eat them in front of it, or to feed the new food to another "flock member" who visibly enjoys it. Merely wanting to join in the "flock's" activity will often be enough to encourage the naturally inquisitive grey to try something new.

**Dishes:** Buy two sets of food and water dishes so that the bird can begin each day with clean bowls.

Water dishes should also be washed whenever the water is dirty. (Some greys like to soak their food.) If a grey is really bad about soaking food or dumping water, supplement that bird's water supply with a drinking tube so that the bird will always have clean water.

## Special Needs

Some greys tend to have low blood calcium, which can lead to seizures and other medical problems. For this reason, it's a good idea to feed calcium-rich foods such as kale, broccoli, Swiss chard, and almonds. Some people supplement calcium with cuttlebone or mineral block in the cage, but many birds chew these up without really swallowing any. Also, cuttlefish can accumulate heavy metal toxins if they come from polluted waters.

A grey's blood calcium level should be checked during its yearly health exams. An experienced avian veterinarian can help to determine what, if any, food supplements might be needed. Don't supplement either vitamins or minerals without a veterinarian's supervision.

## Changing a Bird's Diet

A grey with unhealthy eating habits probably falls into one of these categories:

**1.** It recognizes seed as food and will put nothing else in its mouth.

**2.** It has eaten the same few food items for most of its life and is unwilling to try anything new.

**3.** It has decided what foods it likes and will have temper tantrums until the owner gives it the food it wants.

Birds in the first category cannot be "starved" into eating something they don't consider food any more than a human could be starved into eating marbles. The goal is to get the birds to realize that other things can be eaten. Sprouting their seed is often a good start. Cooking their seed into "omelets" of ½ egg and ½ minced vegetables, or into corn bread that has vegetables in it can encourage them to experiment. Gradually, the seed can be reduced and other ingredients increased in size and quantity. Cooked sweet potatoes or squash or vegetable baby food can be mixed with the seed. Again, other ingredients can be added gradually.

Once the bird is experimenting with new food, or if it is in the second category, the owner can encourage better eating habits by eating in front

*Many birds can be encouraged to try new foods when they see someone else eating them.*

of the bird and sharing. The game for introducing new toys (see page 72) can be helpful. Also, putting made-for-birds skewers with chunks of vegetables near the favorite perch gives the bird a good opportunity to try them. A nearly foolproof method involves replacing the bird's regular food with a new food item for one of their two daily meals every other day. Only one out of four meals is comprised of the new food item, so the bird will only be in danger of eating really well at those meals and in no danger of starving.

Some birds have eaten properly in the past, but are manipulating their owners to give them their favorite food items. Usually, these birds have owners who just want their birds to be happy, so, to accomplish this, they give the bird too much food. Quite often, reducing portions will convince the bird to eat a balanced diet. This is sometimes more effective if the owner feeds the bird, then goes to work so that they need not endure the tantrum.

The bird's weight must be monitored daily when doing dietary changes. Work on a bird's diet only if it is healthy. It is very dangerous to assume that a bird will give in and eat if it is hungry. Extreme changes in the diet may take a year to effect.

### What Not to Feed

Most things that are good for people to eat are suitable for feeding to birds, but these may not be good nutritional choices. Many veterinarians now suggest pellet-only diets because so often the fruits, vegetables, and table food a bird owner feeds turn out to be the low-nutrition choices of apples, corn, and french fries.

- Avocados and chocolate are toxic and should not be fed.
- Caffeine, alcohol, and junk food (foods with high percentages of fat, sugar, or salt) must also be avoided.
- Stale food, old seed, "honey sticks," moldy produce, and other foods that would be rejected by most humans are also unacceptable for birds.

# Grooming

Although grooming is usually necessary to keep an unrestrained companion bird safe in the home, insensitive grooming can adversely affect any bird. Whether it's the result of grooming or the process of grooming, inappropriate trimming of wings, nail, or beak can damage a grey, especially a baby, both physically and emotionally. Either wings that are too short or nails that are too short can cause the bird to fall and crash, which can lead to feather disorders including damaged wing feather follicles and, in extreme cases skin broken open over breastbones.

Grey parrots are heavy-bodied birds that can experience difficulty learning to fly indoors. They must be wing-trimmed in the most noninvasive way possible to prevent uncontrolled and dangerous indoor flight, but not enjoyable flapping.

The following techniques are intended to be minimally invasive, both in the process of grooming and in the effect of grooming on the bird's future confidence and on its ability to comfortably regrow feathers. Even low-stress grooming can be scary for the bird the first time, however, and conditioning to tolerate grooming is an important part of being a responsible parrot owner.

## The Least Invasive Procedure

The least invasive form of companion parrot grooming is trimming only wing feathers without toweling.[1] This ultra-modest grooming technique is especially appropriate for grooming juvenile greys.

Because the grey personality is so sensitive and because these birds obviously demonstrate memory and hold grudges, a new companion grey is best groomed by an outside-the-family professional. Typically, a sensitively administered appropriate wing trim won't produce lingering problems, but if something goes wrong during the process and the bird becomes frightened or panicky, it's best if a familiar human is not associated with the incident. Indeed, if the bird is frightened during grooming, a familiar human should be nearby to rescue the bird from a potentially frightening, unfamiliar situation.

Scissors should be sharp so that they leave smooth edges on the trimmed feathers, which prevents potential feather chewing intended

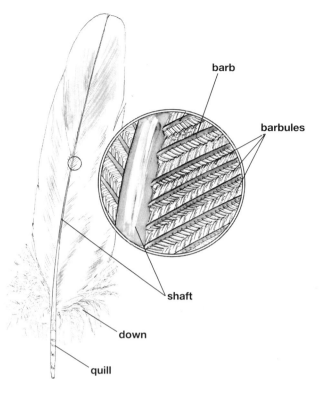

*Tiny filaments called barbules link the barbs that come off the central feather shaft or rachis.*

to "fix" jagged feather edges. Depending upon the bird's age and flight ability, trim only four to seven of the outer primary flight feathers. It's usually best to trim four feathers in younger birds, and up to seven feathers in hearty older birds. Gauge cuts based on how much of the feather extends out of the shorter covering feathers or coverts. For baby greys, trim away about one-third of the part of the first four flight feathers showing from a bone extending beyond the coverts. Older birds and better flyers usually require trimming up to two-thirds of the visible part of the first seven primary feathers extending past the coverts, when the wing is viewed from above or behind.

The bird's wing feathers should fall out (molt) in a symmetrical pattern along the feather tracts (paths of circulation), regrowing two feathers at a time, in mirror image, one on each side. Thus, the feathers molt and regrow symmetrically and the bird retains maximum flight ability.

## The Least Invasive Result

The bird's safety is the primary goal of wing feather trimming; the bird's comfort is the secondary goal. That's why we no longer use trims developed for the poultry industry, such as uneven trimming—cutting all primaries on one wing close or under the coverts and leaving the other wing full—for companion birds. This leaves the bird uncomfortably unbalanced and makes the simple activity of holding onto the top of the cage and flapping difficult and uncomfortable. Young birds, especially, that are trimmed this way may tend to fall in an uncontrolled manner more than symmetrically trimmed birds. Older birds that have been trimmed this way for a long time tend to be inactive, a condition that can contribute to many other physical and behavioral problems.

Secondary feathers should be left intact (see illustration, below) to retain wind resistance so that the bird is able to land, dive, or fall safely. This is an indoor trim for maximum comfort for indoor birds. Birds trimmed as suggested here should be unable to lift off indoors, but not outdoors. No wing trim should be trusted outdoors where a strong gust of wind can blow even a severely trimmed bird away.

If two or three outside primary feathers are left long, they could get caught in cage bars or accessories. In addition, if one feather is molted, then the other mature feather is more vulnerable to being knocked out, leaving a new blood feather coming in completely unprotected.

Low-stress grooming also includes protecting the bird's ability to easily regrow feathers. While some birds seem to tolerate and recover from short trims, other birds have disas-

*Wing feathers should be trimmed carefully. A more restrictive trim is used on very good fliers.*

trous results. Wing feathers that are trimmed up to or under the coverts are especially vulnerable to being knocked out as they molt and regrow one at a time. Each individual blood feather has no protection as it grows past the coverts and can be bent by the simple act of flapping.

*Mature primary feathers protect new feathers as they grow in.*

**Feather Cysts:** Without the protection and support of (partial) feathers on each side, each primary blood feather can be repeatedly broken or knocked out when it grows past the coverts. In greys, feather cysts are usually the result of trauma where the feather grows curled inside the follicle. This can be painful for the bird and can also progress to an inability to regrow these feathers. This condition can produce a sedentary bird that prefers not to use its wings, a bird that chews feathers, or a bird with a phobic or aggressive personality. Inappropriate cage or perches, and overgroomed nails can also contribute to this painful condition.

or other socialization processes; once the new feather regrows completely, it can be trimmed along the same line as the adjacent feathers. Wait for the protective cuticle encasing the feather (when it contains blood supply) to flake away, revealing the completely formed new feather. If you trim the feather before it is completely regrown, you risk cutting the blood supply, in which case the feather would have to be pulled, or having the cut end of the

## Maintaining the Low-Stress Trims

Although early grooming is probably best accomplished by a professional, as the greys become increasingly well-socialized, owners can easily keep up wing trims. In order to prevent frivolous flight, the noninvasive trims must be maintained more carefully than more severe trims. This can be accomplished in the home during towel play

*Unprotected blood feathers can break as they grow in.*

feather continue growing outside the line of the trim. This can be easily remedied by trimming again once the feather has reached full length.

## Grooming Using the Towel Game

While most companion grey parrots will tolerate having the wing feathers groomed without toweling, it may become necessary to wrap the bird in a towel for medical examination or for grooming toenails or beak. If a companion bird has been well conditioned to playing "peek-a-boo" in the towel, then necessary toweling is tremendously easy.

**1.** Begin as you would for the towel game (see page 30). Place the bird on a waist-high perch and approach from below rather than from above as an avian predator would. First, restrict the bird's movement inside the towel, then placing it approximately in the center of the towel, grasp the bird around the neck with one hand, carefully joining the thumb and opposing finger (outside the towel) just under the lower beak. Even if there is a little space in the circle formed by the fingers, if the fingertips meet directly beneath the beak and behind the jawbone, the bird is restrained, and cannot bite.

**2.** Hold the bird's feet with the other hand, being careful not to restrict the in-and-out movement of the breast (a bird has no diaphragm and cannot breathe if the chest cannot expand).

**3.** Once the bird is safely restrained in the towel, a second person can examine the bird, groom wing feathers, toenails, or beak, or perform whatever other procedure is necessary.

## Grooming Without Using the Towel Game

Because grooming can be especially traumatic to an unsocialized bird, early and ongoing socialization to enjoy towel play can help to ensure a happy grooming experience. Occasionally veterinarians will recommend anesthesia for grooming very reactive or uncooperative birds. With a little socialization and sensitive grooming techniques, however, anesthesia is almost always unnecessary for companion greys.

If the bird is not conditioned to accept the towel, the following technique can usually ensure a successful low-stress grooming experience.

**1.** First put the bird on the floor, allowing it to be "herded" into a corner. At this point, just before the towel would be placed over the bird, turn the light out in the room so that the bird doesn't see the "predator" coming.

**2.** Once the bird is safely contained in the towel, turn the light on, and spend some time on sweet words and petting to calm the bird. Practiced and documented-successful petting techniques are especially beneficial here.

**3.** A terrified bird can also sometimes be calmed by making comforting humming or clucking sounds. Be sure not to "shush" or hiss at a screaming, terrified bird; this is what a reptilian predator might do, which could further frighten the bird.

## Grooming Toenails

Although it's extremely important to allow baby grey parrots to have sharp toenails so that they won't fall often and develop related physical and behavioral problems, some grey parrots require frequent toenail grooming. The adult grey parrots' toenails should be kept so that the ball under the end of the toe is not displaced off a flat surface by the length of the nail.

Some birds may be socialized to allow a favorite person to file the tips off the toenails with an emery board, but most birds will probably have to be toweled to have toenails groomed, even by a professional groomer or avian veterinarian.

Most professionals probably prefer a Dremmel tool for grinding African grey toenails. The heat produced by the spinning of the grinding stone can cauterize the blood supply in the toenail as the nail is being groomed, thereby minimizing the risk of bleeding. Occasionally, however, there is a little blood, and care must be taken to ensure that the bleeding is stopped. Use Qwik-Stop coagulating powder rather than a styptic pencil because it is more versatile and less painful.

## Grooming the Beak

Grooming the beak is probably the most stressful part of grooming for most greys. An active, interested grey parrot with sufficient wood available

*Trim any toenail that lifts the end of the toe off of a flat surface.*

of appropriate hardness seldom requires much beak grooming.

Birds that are well acclimated to the towel game often enjoy having their beaks gently filed with a fine emery board by favorite humans. This can seem to the bird like an allopreening interaction. The beaks of unsocialized or uncooperative birds may require professional grooming.

Grey parrots rarely suffer growth deformities of the beak. When they do, it often involves a maxilla (upper beak) growing to one side and a mandible (lower beak) growing to the other side, rather than maxilla and mandible being centered over each other. This condition requires beak reshaping, which must be done gradually and by a professional. Never allow anyone except an experienced professional groomer or veterinarian that the bird tolerates well to use a Dremmel on a grey parrot's beak.

### Applying Grooming Techniques

Low-stress wing and nail trims are used primarily for companion greys, as wing feathers are maintained in more specific and more varied ways for breeding and show situations. These techniques are intended, especially, to ensure the bird's comfort when feathers are regrowing, as the single most common error I see in wing feather trims involves cutting the feathers too short to be able to regrow with protection.

Unfortunately, when travelling around the country for educational events, we often see grey parrots, especially, enduring painfully difficult feather growth situations including acquired tendency to wing feather cysts and a breast that is repeatedly split open by falls because flight

*A grey's beak should have enough of a point left so it can still use it for climbing, even after grooming.*

feathers were trimmed up to or under the coverts. Especially for African greys, an effective wing trim doesn't have to be short, it just has to be kept up-to-date.

# Potty-training the Fastidious Grey Parrot

African greys are known as the most fastidious of parrots. It's not unusual for a companion African grey parrot to refuse to defecate while inside its roost cage. A grey parrot might choose to eliminate in only one or two areas of the regular daytime cage, or it might not eliminate in any chosen territory at all. This behavior, like several others we've discussed here, is probably a result of the numerous predators that wild grey parrots must so carefully avoid.

It can be quite a shock when a new parrot owner suddenly notices that the bird has some sort of "protocol" for eliminating. That protocol will vary from bird to bird, but usually remains consistent in a particular grey parrot as long as that bird has no reason to change. Parrot behavioral consultants come across questions about the greys, elimination habits with great regularity. Following is a sample of these questions.

**• Why won't my grey parrot eliminate in the cage where it sleeps?**
The cautious grey parrot is probably too smart to eliminate where it

sleeps in the wild so that predators are not attracted to the roosting areas.

• **Will it hurt my grey parrot if I sleep too long?**

If the bird is not free-fed (see section on Diet, page 80), it will not be taking in food during the hours of human sleep. If the bird is given the same amount of food every evening, then about the same amount of waste will accumulate. Holding it a little longer shouldn't be a problem for a sleeping bird. If the bird develops a sense of safety, and humans sleep for very long periods, the bird will discontinue the fastidious behavior.

• **Why won't my grey parrot eliminate anyplace in the cage except where it naps?**

A particular grey parrot probably naps during the day in a site close to where it forages. This is perceived to be far enough from the roost to seem safe; it has been observed that grey parrots may have to fly 20 or more miles (30-plus km) daily to find food. In captivity, nap sites are probably less numerous and so it will be easily observable where the bird has chosen to eliminate.

• **What can I do to change this behavior?**

There is usually no reason to change this behavior, except by exploiting it for potty-training the bird. If the bird is extremely fastidious and must remain caged for very long periods, it might benefit from the introduction of a roost cage inside a much larger daytime cage. Use different substrate in each cage so that the bird can easily determine a difference in the territory.

## How to Potty-train Your Bird

It's tremendously easy to reinforce natural, self-rewarding behavior; eliminating is both natural and self-rewarding. It's probably quite a bit easier to potty-train a grey parrot than a puppy. And, if you decide not to potty-train your grey—it does add stress, and may not be appropriate for very sensitive birds—the waste is water-soluble and not especially smelly. If you do decide to potty-train a companion grey, you can easily take advantage of the bird's natural instincts to eliminate in particular areas just as it is picked up.

Grey parrots have a reputation for being cautious. Some birds seem to frequently appear on the verge of flying away. Because they need to be as light as possible for flying, they have a natural instinct to eliminate before they fly. If the bird is nervous, it will eliminate from this motivation even if its wing feathers are trimmed and it cannot fly away, or if it has never had the experience of flying. This behavior probably makes potty-training a grey parrot easier than other birds that are less often stimulated by shyness to flight. Combined with their fastidious toilet habits, these two natural behaviors make many grey parrots almost naturally potty-trained.

Simply pick up the bird and hold it over approved substratum, such

*Some greys avoid defecating inside their own cages.*

as a newspaper; the bird's natural instincts will probably stimulate defecation. If the bird is not put down and picked up again, you should have at least 20 to 30 minutes or so before the urge to eliminate will be strong again. Put the bird down in a place where it does not customarily eliminate, then pick it up again to stimulate it to defecate over the newspaper.

You can control when and where the bird eliminates. Each time it is picked up or passed from one person to another, expect it to eliminate. Be prepared to hold it over newspaper, and verbally reinforce the behavior. This method is also the easiest way to potty-train *Poicephalus* parrots and cockatoos.

## The Visual Stimulus: Substratum

Dr. Susan Clubb reports that newspaper with print is the best material to use to line the bottom of bird cages. The ink in the newspaper appears to retard the growth of bacteria, fungus, and molds more than any other material tested. Newspaper is an ideal visual stimulus for teaching a grey parrot where to eliminate. If the approved areas for eliminating are lined with newspaper, and if the bird is reinforced to eliminate when you hold it over newspaper, then the bird is well on its way to being "potty-trained."

When handling or playing with the bird in a place you do not wish soiled with droppings, watch for tail movements that might indicate that the bird wants to eliminate, or keep an eye on the clock and put the bird down for a few minutes every 20 or 30 minutes. A well-socialized bird might eliminate immediately when put down and immediately want to be picked up again. If this doesn't happen, stop eye contact and look for signs that the bird's interest has shifted from you and what you're doing to something else; maybe watch the bird wag its tail or preen for a few seconds, or bop a bell, or take a drink. Be sure there's been a break in the intellectual and emotional connection with the bird. Wait a few minutes, then pick the bird up and solicit interaction, hold it over newspaper, and the bird will eliminate before becoming emotionally "connected" again.

If this doesn't occur, try waiting a few minutes longer before putting the bird down, leaving the bird down a few minutes longer, giving a small food treat before picking the bird up, or encouraging a little wing flapping just as you pick the bird up. Any one of these activities could stimulate a grey parrot to eliminate. Reinforce the bird with verbal praise when it does.

Within a very short time, possibly a few days or a week, the grey parrot, whether it is young or old, usually gets a strong notion of where it should and should not eliminate. Only the neighborhood dry cleaners and carpet cleaners will be disappointed.

[1] Mattie Sue Athan, *Guide to Companion Parrot Behavior*, Hauppauge, NY: Barron's Educational Series, Inc., 1999.

## Chapter Six

# Medical Care

The grey parrots' instinct to live in flocks dictates that they can mask signs of illness. This means that a African grey parrot can look perfectly healthy while harboring an illness that will not be revealed until later. Often, the stress of going to a new home can bring out symptoms of disease that had previously remained hidden. A bird owner has the responsibility to ensure that this new friend is healthy and robust. Anyone who purchases a parrot should insist on a health guarantee that allows enough time to visit an avian veterinarian and to obtain test results, usually from one to two weeks.

# Choosing an Avian Veterinarian

A veterinarian must have much more than a passing interest in birds to stay abreast of recent developments. Avian veterinary science is a rapidly expanding field. Avian veterinarians must frequently continue their education in this field in order to practice it competently. Look for a board-certified avian veterinarian; there are a few. Otherwise, look for a member of the Association of Avian Veterinarians (see Useful Addresses and Literature, page 165). In most urban areas, an avian veterinarian will have a clientele that is more than 50 percent birds and/or exotics. Also ask if the veterinarian has taken a test showing proficiency in this area. Ask for references and check them.

## The Veterinary Examination

An initial examination allows the new parrot owner to be more confident of the bird's good health. Even if the bird comes from a reputable source, there are illnesses such as Psittacine Beak or Feather Disease that cannot be detected without diagnostic tests.

This is an excellent time for the veterinarian to become familiar with the individual bird. While there are books and charts telling what data is considered normal for different kinds of birds, there are variations between individuals. The veterinarian will obtain valuable information about what is normal for a particular bird by seeing that bird when it is normal. Build a sound relationship with the veterinarian at the beginning. An emergency is the worst possible time for a pet owner to decide he or she doesn't feel comfortable with the doctor.

An avian veterinarian might recommend annual or semiannual examinations for a particular bird. Regular examinations can help to identify health problems in their early stages. This is particularly useful if you have only a few birds and might not otherwise be in regular contact with a veterinarian. The veterinarian remains familiar with the bird and potential health problems can be identified through changes that occur too slowly for you to notice.

## Vaccinations

As avian medicine expands and progresses, new developments in prevention such as vaccines are beginning to become available. There are several vaccines on the market, but some may be too new or risky for veterinarians to recommend. Others have proven safe and effective. Veterinarians may suggest vaccinations on an individual case basis; however, there are no standard immunizations suggested for African grey parrots.

## Signs of Illness

Greys that are well cared for rarely become sick. Proper diet, clean, uncrowded conditions, exercise,

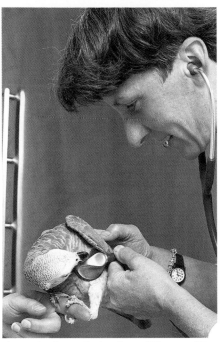

*A good avian veterinarian will be sensitive when examining the parrot.*

fresh air, and a low-stress life allow the bird to maintain a healthy immune system and will help it to resist infections caused by common bacteria and viruses. Crowded birds with poor diets, living in stressful conditions, may have chronic disease problems. Very young and very old parrots are more susceptible to diseases. Unweaned birds and newly weaned birds have less resistance to disease than mature birds with fully developed immune systems.

A wise parrot keeper monitors behavior, droppings, and weight to help determine a parrot's health. Changes in these three areas can indicate possible illness.

## Behavior

Greys have a general activity level that remains relatively consistent. The bird will have napping, playing, and vocalizing times, as well as times when it is more affectionate. Noticeable variations in these patterns, particularly if the bird is more quiet and less active than usual, can indicate possible health issues. Some birds may seem more agitated or jumpy; some may be more affectionate when they don't feel well.

The best time to assess the bird's activity level is when you are not paying direct attention to the bird. In nature, predators watch for sick or injured animals because they are easier to catch. If a bird were to act sick for minor illnesses or discomforts, it would not live to reproduce because predators would attack. Also, the other birds in the flock might drive an obviously sick bird away to prevent disease transmission to the rest of the flock. For these reasons, even a bird that doesn't feel well is likely to act normal when interacting with its human. In many instances, you must be aware that something doesn't seem "quite right" about the bird.

Don't wait more than a day or two. If the bird doesn't improve, especially if it is getting noticeably worse, you should stop waiting and take the bird to the veterinarian. You know the bird better than anyone else. An experienced bird veterinarian will not always expect a bird owner to be able to describe specific symptoms and will trust your judgment, whether or not you can identify specific complaints. While a list of symptoms is extremely helpful in diagnosing a problem, it is not always possible to come up with one. It is safer to have the bird checked than to wait until it is too late.

**Droppings:** There are three parts to the bird's droppings.

**1.** Normal feces (the "green" part) will appear homogenous, well digested, and worm-like. Feces should usually have a firm consistency and should contain no distinguishable pieces of food. Color may change with the food consumed. Fresh fruits and vegetables can make droppings loose and sloppy; this should not be mistaken for diarrhea. When a bird has pellets as the base of its diet, stools should return to normal consistency after a pelleted meal.

**2.** The white part of the droppings carries the nitrogenous wastes and is called the *urates*. The urates of a healthy bird will be separate from the other two parts and will be opaque white. Occasionally, the whites will be temporarily stained from something the bird ate. Lime green or mustard yellow could indicate liver problems. Kidney problems can keep the bird from properly forming urates so that the liquid part of the dropping is cloudy white. Any observable change in urates or feces lasting more than a day or two is good reason to consult a veterinarian.

**3.** The third part of the stool is liquid urine. It is usually clear and colorless, although it can pick up some color along with the feces. The amount of urine varies with the amount of water contained in the food or the amount of water the bird has consumed. Stress can cause the bird to have droppings that consist only of clear fluid; this should not be confused with diarrhea. Sometimes there will be more water in stools in summer because birds drink more water when the weather is hot. A change in the amount of liquid in the stool is probably no cause for concern unless it is extreme and ongoing.

Diarrhea in a parrot shows up as undigested food in the feces, droppings that do not have three distinct parts, and weight loss in the bird. Whenever you believe an African grey has diarrhea, you should take the bird to the veterinarian as soon as possible. True diarrhea generally requires medical attention if the bird is to survive.

**Weight:** Unless an African grey parrot is on a diet, any noticeable weight loss is cause for immediate veterinary attention. Determining whether or not a bird has lost weight cannot be done by looking at the bird or by holding it on your hand. The best way to determine weight loss is to weigh the bird in the morning before it eats. Otherwise, examine the bird's keel bone frequently. The keel is a flat bone that is attached perpendicular to the sternum, below the bird's crop. The bird's flight muscles are attached to this protruding bone. Flight muscles are the largest muscles in the bird's body; they accurately reflect the loss of muscle tissue that occurs when a bird loses weight.

Feeling the keel bone on a regular basis will allow you to become familiar with the parrot's normal physical shape. If the keel bone becomes more prominent, you should contact the veterinarian. If the keel bone gets harder to find due to surrounding flesh, the bird should probably (under veterinary approval) be fed less. If you are actually weighing the bird, look for a decrease of 10 percent or more. Birds do not go on diet and exercise programs of their own accord. Weight loss in a pet bird is a serious matter that requires an avian veterinarian's care and cannot be remedied by feeding the bird more.

## Other Symptoms

**1.** Sneezing can indicate a sinus infection, or the bird could be modeling a human sneeze, or it could just be a reaction to dry air.

**2.** Regurgitating could be a crop infection or a sign of true love.

**3.** Feather plucking or chewing could have its basis in a medical problem or in behavior.

**4.** Coughing usually occurs shortly after someone in the house has had a cold. African grey parrots do not cough. They do, however, do an excellent imitation of a human coughing.

It never hurts to call the veterinarian if there is a question concerning the parrot's health. It can be fatal to wait to see if the health problem will go away or if it will worsen.

### The Broken Blood Feather

A bird's new feathers are formed outside its body in a tapered spike. The bluish part of this spike contains the blood supply. As it grows, a fully developed feather will protrude from the end of the spike. The sheath that formed the spike dries up and flakes off; this is the source of much bird dust or dander. Every feather on the bird's body, including the down feathers, began as "blood" or "pin" feathers.

Blood feathers are normal structures and do not usually pose a problem unless they are broken.

Grey parrots can break blood feathers when they flap their wings against something or if they fall. A broken blood feather is usually either a wing or a tail feather. If the bird has broken a blood feather while flapping its wings, there will most likely be blood splattered on the walls. In this instance, a little blood can look like a lot. Don't panic. Usually the problem is not as bad as it looks and the feather will have already stopped bleeding.

The first time this happens, take the bird immediately to an experi-

*Every feather that is commonly seen begins as a blood feather.*

enced avian veterinarian, behavioral consultant, groomer, or grey breeder. They can demonstrate how to safely deal with the blood feather. One person will first restrain the bird in a towel. With the affected area exposed, the feather can be inspected. Blood may be coming from the tip of the blood feather or from a crack in the sheath. If the feather is cracked, it cannot form a normal feather and must be pulled out. Also, the shaft will be very weak and will easily start bleeding again. If the end of the feather is leaking blood, this will often heal itself, possibly leaving a stress mark, and will not need to be pulled unless a large amount of blood is being lost.

To remove the feather, grasp as much of the base of the feather shaft as possible using needle-nose pliers or a hemostat. The base of the feather inside the skin should be supported firmly with one hand while the other hand pulls the feather straight out in the direction it grows. If the entire feather is successfully extracted, the end of the shaft will be rounded with a small hole at the tip. There will be a little blood coming from the follicle where the feather came out. Apply pressure with your fingers, pressing the follicle closed; the bleeding will usually stop within one or two minutes.

Occasionally, the feather will be broken off too near the skin and there will not be enough of the shaft left to pull the feather out. In this case, if the feather is still bleeding, a styptic or clotting agent can be used to stop the bleeding. Sometimes the end of the wing itself may be bleeding. Styptic powder ("Qwik Stop") should not be used on skin. A weak solution of Betadine should be used to clean the affected area. Apply pressure until the bleeding stops. In extreme cases, the wing should be bandaged. This should be done by an avian veterinarian.

**Causes:** Sometimes the cage is the problem, or how the bird uses it. Toys and perches must be arranged so that the bird doesn't bump into them when flapping. A diet deficient in certain nutrients can cause blood feathers to be abnormally weak. Most broken blood feathers on the wings of companion greys are probably the result of too-short wing trims that have left too little support for regrowing feathers (see Grooming on page 86).

**Note:** Although most broken blood feathers do not require a trip to the veterinarian, if the bird is excessively lethargic or stressed it may have lost a lot of blood and may require medical care. Things should be perfectly normal by the next day. A grey parrot with frequent broken blood feathers should be seen by a veterinarian, as this could indicate a tendency to develop feather cysts or other problems.

# Transmitting Diseases Between Humans and Birds

Most illnesses cannot be transmitted from birds to humans or the other way around. Many birds are probably more disease-resistant than their human companions. If a bird gets a cold at the same time as a human, it may be a coincidence due to environmental factors. Seasonal "colds" can seem to be transmitted from human to bird, although the same conditions that stress a human's immune system can also stress a bird's.

In general, different types of bacteria are infectious to birds than to humans. Both humans and birds can be affected by salmonella or *E. coli* and both humans and birds can get ornithosis. Ornithosis, which was previously called psittacosis or parrot fever can be transmitted between humans and birds. Transmission to humans is extremely rare and usually is considered to be an occupational disease of those working around birds. However, persons with pneumonialike symptoms should tell their doctor that they own a parrot in order to assist in diagnosing this easily curable disease.

### What Should Not Be Done for a Sick or Injured Bird

It's very difficult to sit and wait while a beloved companion is suffering. African grey keepers must be cautioned against taking matters into their own hands. Here's a list of things *not* to do:
• Don't give over-the-counter medication.
• Don't give medication that has been previously prescribed for the bird or for anyone else.
• Don't attempt procedures that are unfamiliar.
• Don't apply any creams, sprays, or oil-based ointments.

## Injuries

You can treat a minor injury in the case of a nicked toe or wing tip. Applying a weak solution of Betadine will keep the area from becoming infected. If there is much bleeding or if the injury involved another pet, a trip to the veterinarian is called for. Sterile gauze and slight pressure can be applied to a bleeding wound. Scratches from other animals usually require antibiotics.

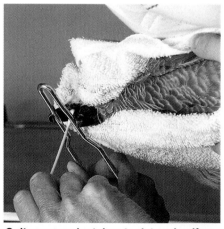

*Cultures may be taken to determine if an infection is present.*

## Home Emergency Kit

- Coagulant—first-aid powder to stop bleeding.
- Pedialyte or Lactated Ringers—replacement of electrolytes in dehydrated or sick birds.
- Hemostat or needle-nose pliers—to pull out broken blood feathers.
- Betadine—to disinfect any bleeding wound.
- Carrier—to be kept handy in case of fire or other emergency.
- Towel—to restrain the bird, if necessary.
- Heating pad—to keep the bird warm, when necessary.
- Sterile gauze—to bind wounds, if necessary.
- Scissors—to cut the sterile gauze.

If you suspect a broken bone or concussion, you should keep the bird as still as possible and take it to an emergency facility. Do not try to stabilize the injured part, as this can make the injury worse.

# Holistic Medicine

Traditional Western avian medicine sometimes falls short when it comes to subtle and difficult-to-diagnose health conditions in parrots. Many reliable aviculturists report that their birds have had their lives saved by acupuncture, homeopathy, or Chinese herbs.

Holistic medicine is targeted more to prevention than treatment. A strong body does not get sick. Companion parrots on a holistic regimen involving diet and low stress appear healthier and happier. Additionally, if there is a disease present, holistic treatment is usually less invasive and is both less dangerous and less stressful to the bird. In places where it is available, holistic avian medicine is obviously a viable alternative that can be seen to save lives.

# Before You See a Veterinarian

**1.** A sick or injured bird should be kept warm and still so that the parrot can use its energy to fight the illness or heal its injury. A bird's body temperature is higher than ours, often around 105°F (40.6°C). Much of a bird's energy goes to maintaining this temperature. A covered cage with a heating pad under or on the side is an excellent idea.

**2.** Save the newspapers from the bottom of the cage so that the veterinarian can assess the droppings.

**3.** Transport the bird in a carrier or a box with ventilation. If the bird is panting, the temperature in the carrier is too high.

## Chapter Seven
# Behavioral Issues

Greys, like many other parrots, have the ability to allow humans to take the place of birds in the roles of mates and flock members. This is a fairly unique ability among wild animals. The bird's behavior must be guided and nurtured. This is the most effective way to teach the grey parrot to be a happy, socially acceptable member of our society. Unfortunately many misunderstandings can arise when humans and birds try to form an alliance. Since humans are the more adaptable of the two it is up to us to design interactions to be as understandable to the bird as possible.

## Unfulfilled Needs

Interflock relationships, mate relationships, foraging, nesting, escaping, seasonal cycles, and breeding cycles are among the drives and desires parrots are innately equipped to experience. A companion grey is under stress simply from not being able to participate in these experiences. Filling all those needs in captivity is virtually impossible. Additionally, having to deal with being confined in a house or a cage, having to learn ways to self-reward—something parrots *never* have to worry about in the wild—overstimulation, understimulation, and having to learn how to be a parrot from a totally different species are all situations that grey parrots are not naturally equipped to deal with. It's a wonder they can cope at all.

While we can try to give our grey parrots as full a life as possible, it is not to our benefit to think that we are providing everything they require. As soon as we decide that we have provided for them completely, we deny ourselves the opportunity to learn new ways to accommodate our exotic friends more adequately.

## Copying Behavior

The strongest and smartest greys get the best food, the best nest sites, and the mate of choice. These individuals are held in high regard by other flock members that watch and copy their behavior. A successful relationship between human and companion grey parrot casts the human in the role of "leader," with the inherent responsibility of setting a good example for other members of the flock. Humans gain status in a parrot's eyes when they take time to model, guide, and reinforce appropriate behavior. If a particular human doesn't spend at least a little time teaching the bird appropriate behavior, then the bird might not see that human as a valued member of the flock, and might try to drive that human away.

A young parrot expects to have its behavior guided and instinctually knows to learn from dominant flock members what behaviors are acceptable. It's not unusual for a grey parrot to abuse a human who talks sweetly but fails to demonstrate higher status in flock "society."

## Stimulating and Rewarding Good Behavior

Verbal (or vocal) cues in conjunction with body language are the easiest ways to communicate praise to a parrot. Grey parrots can easily be conditioned to respond in predictable ways when certain words are used repeatedly in similar situations. Body language and tone of voice are as important as using the words in context frequently.

The phrase "*Good bird*" is useful to teach a bird, but it must be given as much meaning in the context of the interaction as possible. This is similar to a person watching "Star Trek" and listening to Klingons. We

*This African grey is begging to be included in the "flock" activities.*

can pick up that a certain series of sounds signifies the end of a conversation. We don't know whether a literal translation would be "See you later" or "Your grandmother has nice teeth," but we can pick up the context and whether the words have an emotional effect for either party. In the same way, the bird may not understand the moral implications of being good, but it will seek the acceptance being offered by the other flock member and can associate that with the words being said.

Laughter, "*Good bird*," and "*Pretty bird*" are all examples of things that a grey will perceive as praise (reinforcement). The best results come when the words you choose to praise your bird with are used with enthusiasm. If the bird does not pay attention when you say the words, then the praise probably isn't getting through. The bird should at least make eye con-

tact, possibly with only one eye. Preferably, the bird's eyes will pinpoint; it will move its head forward and slightly down, maybe cock its head to one side. The bird's feathers will be slightly fluffy, so that the edges of the scalloped chest and neck feathers may take on a ruffled look. The bird might lift its foot to solicit being picked up. These are all indications of friendly intent and clues that the grey parrot is accepting your praise and reinforcement. If the bird doesn't react, you should add enthusiasm, include games and "Peek-a-boos," or increase volume until the bird shows interest.

When adequately reinforced, praise can come before an action. Many times a bird will say "*Good bird*" just before performing appropriately. In this way, praise can represent a prompt. If you suspect the bird is considering misbehaving, particularly if there might be a reason to misbehave, such as to get your attention, you can say "*Good bird*" before the bird misbehaves. The bird may realize it has your attention so no further action is required, or it may be distracted long enough to change its mind.

Another word that can easily be established as a cue is "*Careful*." If a baby grey parrot is told at times when it might fall, or drop something, or lose footing to "*Be careful*," the bird can learn that these words mean that something it doesn't want to happen might happen. If you can anticipate unwanted behavior, a well-patterned parrot can be influ-

*This bird's almond shaped eyes and relaxed feathers show his friendly intent.*

enced to avoid the unwanted behavior simply with the use of the words *"Be careful."*

# Anticipate, Distract, and Reinforce

Once cues have been established, they can be used to distract from unwanted behavior. When we see a misbehavior coming—maybe a nip during step-ups—we can't just say *"No."* Many birds enjoy the drama of this exchange; others might perceive two opposite messages: *"Step-up!"* and *"No."* What's a bird to do?

We can say to the bird *"Are you going to be a good bird?"* Combined with eye contact, this technique can prevent misbehavior by reminding the bird not only of what is expected, but also of how it feels to enjoy the attention associated with the buzz words. It also reinforces the bird's sense that humans are in charge.

It's difficult at first not to say *"No," "Don't," or "Stop"* when a painfully sharp beak is closed or nearly closed around your finger; it goes against the way most humans would naturally respond. But changes in human/bird interactions must begin with humans. If humans can be trained to use words or body language to more effectively distract the bird, then the bird can be trained not to nip. A well-reinforced behavioral response provides a sense of security for the bird because it

knows what will happen next. Almost any familiar interaction can be patterned.

Anything that the bird has done once can be reinforced. Life is fun, and all creatures prefer to do things they enjoy. Since almost any nonviolent interaction with a human might be interpreted by the bird to be reinforcement, we must take care not to allow unwanted behaviors to occur. For example, if the bird is nipping in response to a particular set of interactions, you must redesign the way those interactions are performed. If the bird is nipping hands as it is coming off the cage, you might choose to temporarily step-up the bird off the cage onto hand-held perches (see page 11), or stop letting the bird stand on top of the cage. You might use the Good Hand/Bad Hand technique—distract the bird's eyes just before giving the step-up command—or you might have the bird step-up onto towel-covered hands.

It's quite common to accidentally reinforce behavior, especially in a creature that is looking for any kind of attention (reward). As we have mentioned, even saying *"No"* can provide drama or excitement. A normal, creative parrot trained to anticipate praise (reward) for good behavior usually becomes more willing to seek new ways to generate rewards. The bird will also gradually abandon behaviors that do not bring at least occasional reinforcement. Reinforcement includes anything the bird enjoys. Verbal praise, a treat, a kiss on the beak, or a head scratch make very effective rewards.

## Punishments and "Quick Fixes"

Because of the grey parrot's sensitive nature and well-developed fight-or-flight response, there is no such thing as an effective punishment for a grey. Because it is a prey species, the bird's natural tendency to avoid danger must be respected. The effects of both punishments and reprimands are so counterproductive that even the mildest punishments are to be absolutely avoided. A nipping young grey is not to be dropped, forcefully squirted, thumped on the beak, isolated in a scary place, or hit in any way. Even if a reprimand temporarily or permanently causes the bird to discontinue the unwanted behavior, the potential for damaging the bird or the human/bird bond is very real. Additionally, even if a bird is not immediately affected by a reprimand, damaging behavioral response can appear later.

Distracting to appropriate behavior and positive reinforcement are the best means of modifying unwanted grey behavior. This is absolutely the easiest way to train a grey parrot. It is often successfully employed even though humans may be unaware of what they are doing. It's just as common for someone to be accidentally reinforcing good behaviors as it is to be accidentally reinforcing unwanted ones.

We must not consider a recently introduced change to be a permanent change. Even step-ups can be considered a "quick fix" if they are done only occasionally. The benefit of an immediate behavioral change can be the turning point in the attitudes of humans who create the bird's behavioral environment, even if it isn't automatically a permanent change. It can be difficult to change human behavior. Anything that can safely generate a one-time change, even "quick fixes," can demonstrate what a companion bird is capable of and may be the best way to convince humans that if they change *their* ways, the bird's behavior will also change.

There is probably a window of opportunity of three to five days to reinforce introduced and newly improvised behavioral changes in most grey parrots. If the changes are not almost immediately reinforced into patterns, the behavior will return to what it was before.

# Biting

Parrots in the wild seldom bite each other. Biting appears in companion parrots as improvised behavior that has been reinforced into a habit. In addition to reinforcing the behavior with repetition, a person who is being repeatedly bitten during interactions with a grey parrot might be acting too confrontational and not inspirational enough. That is, humans must learn to appropriately encourage their companion parrots how to behave.

## Common Causes of Biting

If it seems that a bird is learning to bite, you must shift gears—distract it to other behavior—so that you can prevent reinforcement of biting into a pattern. Most bites can probably be placed in one of three categories. It's easier to stimulate successful distractions from the biting, if you first understand which kind of biting we are seeing.

**1.** Fear or anxiety biting is the first part of the fight-or-flight response.
• Be less confrontational.
• Improve access to feelings of safety.
• Don't force the bird out of the cage.
• Improve cooperation patterning using the towel game, eye games, or other nonthreatening strategies.
• Model cooperative behavior.

**2.** Territorial biting to defend a mate, status, toys, nest site, height, food, or water supply. This includes displaced aggression, which is biting something or someone the bird can reach out and bite when it cannot reach the individual it wants to bite.
• Watch for signs of territorial biting.
• Maintain eye contact
• Put the bird down or handle it with hand-held perches or with the towel game.
• Improve step-up patterning and bonding with increased handling and outings.

**3.** Manipulation biting, learned behavior intended to get one's way, such as biting when the owner looks away, is on the phone, or when returning the bird to the cage.

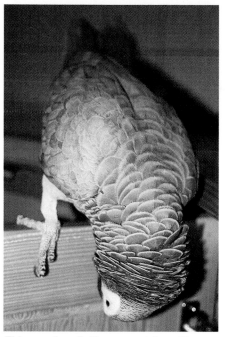

*This grey is soliciting a scratch and is unlikely to bite.*

• Avoid opportunities for the bird to engage in these behaviors, and therefore, to have these behaviors reinforced.
• Don't stop eye contact when answering the phone or returning the bird to the cage. Put the bird down before answering the phone. Behaviors that are not engaged in cannot be reinforced into habits.
• Again, continue handling with hand-held perches or with the towel game.
• Improve step-up patterning.

## What to Do If a Grey Parrot Bites You

Of course, the best way to deal with biting is to prevent it, but if all efforts have failed and you are looking down at a grey parrot lacerating your flesh and unwilling to stop lacerating your flesh, what do you do?

Deter suggests that if the bird is sitting on your hand or on a perch, it's pretty easy to get the bird to release by pushing the hand being bitten down and toward the bird. Of course, this is absolutely counterintuitive. Anyone who knows how human reflexes work probably knows that most humans experiencing a painful bite want to pull their hand away. If you pull away, you run the risk of ripping flesh, injuring the bird, or actually teaching the bird to bite by a response that will reinforce the behavior.

In addition to a gentle distracting wobble (see page 49), you may see some relief by putting the bird quickly, gently, and unceremoniously on the floor. Some birds will release if light-blocking fabric is placed over their heads. If the bird is hanging on and grinding, you might try forcing something else into the beak, deflecting the bird to bite down on a magazine or another object.

Eye contact is really important, here, for often if you can catch the bird's eye, it will release the bite. A manufactured distraction may be necessary to change the determined bird's focus on the bite. That could mean clapping the other hand against your thigh or suddenly turning the television volume up with the remote.

# Unwanted Vocalizations

Unwanted vocalizations in grey parrot homes involve a different type of sound than that encountered in most other parrot households. A grey parrot's alarm calls can be ear piercing and are difficult for some humans to tolerate. Intrusive sounds can be artfully used by a creative grey parrot to intentionally annoy humans or merely to get their attention.

## Learned Behaviors

In addition to possessing a few truly disturbing calls, greys have a natural attraction to sounds that fall within the natural range of their voices. A modern companion grey can do variations on all types of electronic tones: microwave, alarm clock, computer, oven timer, car alarm, smoke detector, and telephone answering machine, among others. The most common noise complaint among grey parrots involves birds' either natural alarm signals or learned electronic alarms as attention-demanding behavior.

Attention-demanding noise commonly occurs when humans try to talk on the phone, talk to each other, leave the room, or watch television. The tones are designed as alarms to remind humans to do something. When humans hear one of these beeps or tones, they usually are stimulated to jump up and rush around. It seems to be quite amusing to a bird to be able to make humans jump up and run around. Of course, the best way to prevent the development of attention-demanding noises in grey parrots is to ignore the behaviors when they first appear. A behavior that is not reinforced usually disappears.

Both signaling and "singing" can be self-rewarding behavior. Beeps and whistles also seem to function as a part of singing in some grey parrots. These birds will sing at regular times such as dinnertime and bright sunny mornings when others are singing and showering. These calls might be used in a sort of nervous way, when something isn't quite right, or they might be used to get attention. Birds that are using electronic tones as attention-demanding behaviors might scream out when the owner leaves the room, sits down, answers the phone, or tries to read, write, or work. Birds that are using these calls in a nervous way will settle down when necessary changes are made.

Of course, there are times when alarm calls and loud vocalizations are appropriate. If the bird's needs are not being met, or if there is danger, the bird has every right to try to attract as much attention as necessary. If an otherwise quiet bird is making a fuss, investigate; there could be no water, dirty water, a cat, a mouse, or a fire. Sometimes, the bird is just trying to tell us something.

## Preventing Profanity

While the screaming parrot may present a problem for neighbors, frequent or untimely obscenities can adversely affect the quality of a bird's life by annoying humans in its own home. Foul-mouthed birds may be increasingly isolated and left to gradually lose interest in interactions with humans. They are often banned from exciting outings and social interactions with honored guests.

Probably the most common nuisance word or phrase for a companion parrot to acquire is an occasional obscenity, "*Hot damn*" or "*Darn*" or more colorful expressions that most of us would not repeat in front of parents, children, or too-interested social workers. A parrot doesn't quite spontaneously invent words, although it can happen; the bird is usually copying some sound it relates to. So how did those particular words or sounds wind up coming out of this bird? The bird is mimicking what it heard. Some humans seem truly unaware that they are

*Greys will often tilt their heads when concentrating on a sound they intend to imitate.*

## Peek-a-boo

The client was obviously distressed. His neighbor had gone out of town for the weekend, leaving him to baby-sit a hen cockatiel. Within 48 hours, Bird—his only bird, a beautiful Red-tailed grey parrot—would utter no sound but the shrieking alarm signal of the female cockatiel.

This man knew that the behavior could more likely be changed sooner than later. He called a professional immediately indicating a need for emergency behavioral assistance.

Stepping off the elevator, I could hear the shrieking call through the closed door at the end of the hallway. It sounded exactly like the most excruciatingly annoying hen cockatiel "*CHIRP!*" I had ever heard, except it was about three times louder.

Remaining out of sight of the bird, I asked, "How long has this been going on?"

"Well, this is Wednesday," the soft-spoken owner replied. "I baby-sat my neighbor's cockatiel from Friday through Sunday. This started Monday morning, and I called you before noon that day."

"Well, we should be able to fix this pretty easily, then. Please bring me two solid-colored towels, preferably gray."

Entering the room, we were careful not to look at the bird when it chirped for attention. We sat across the room from each other, draping large gray terry cloth towels over our heads so that our faces as well as our heads were obscured. Then we spent about 30 or 40 minutes playing "Peek-a-boo" with the towels, around the corners of the room, and from behind the furniture.

Almost immediately upon seeing this unusual human behavior, Bird discontinued that newly acquired chirp. In true grey parrot fashion, he remained absolutely motionless for quite a few minutes. Close examination revealed that only his body was motionless. His eyes were pinpointing like crazy, and within about ten minutes, he was back to making occasional normal, happy, grey parrot clicks when he seemed especially delighted. We were observing quite a few bright-red tail wags, and I went home feeling optimistic about our progress.

The owner reported later that by the next morning, Bird was saying "*Peek-a-boo*" any time he could get a little attention—and even sometimes when he could not! He completely forgot about that annoying cockatiel sound.

MSA

saying the words that their birds are repeating.

There are at least two components to the establishment of habitual behavior: enactment (doing the behavior) and reinforcement (being rewarded for enacting the behavior). Even if a bird has learned to speak a human word, the word will not be repeated frequently if the bird is not rewarded, usually with attention, for saying the word.

## Replacing Unwanted Behavior

The easiest way to get a bird to discontinue saying something is by getting it to say or do something else. Try to determine what cues the bird to say the word. Divert the bird to a different word or behavior before the unwanted words or sounds are made. If the word or sound appeared only recently, often, simply ignoring the behavior will eliminate it.

**Remodeling:** Something I call "remodeling" is another valuable device that can be easily used to vanquish new nuisance words. If the bird is saying, for example, "*Damn it!*" we can often divert the pronunciation of the newly acquired word to something like "*Can it!*" This can be done either as a spontaneous response to the word or as a planned distraction before the use of the offensive word.

Remodeling can be combined with use of the model/rival method, which is often described by Dr. Irene Pepperberg in her work with Alex.

This process involves setting up a competitive situation in which a human or other bird rival is rewarded for saying a more desirable word or pronunciation. If the bird says "*Damn it!*" and is not rewarded, and the rival bird or human assistant says "*Can it*" and *is* rewarded, then the bird, seeking to be rewarded, will learn to say "*Can it.*"

## Habitual or Established Vocalizations

If a behavior has been repeated for about 21 days, there is a good chance that it has become habitual; that is, it has become an established part of the bird's routine behavior. A bird that has been habitually repeating a nuisance phrase or sound for a few months or a few years will be a more difficult challenge than a bird that has only recently started repeating an expletive. A parrot will remember things it said years ago, just as you can remember how to say a word that you may not have spoken in many years, and just as you can remember how to play Monopoly and ride a bicycle, although you may not have done those things for quite some time. However, if there is sufficient reason not to say or do those old things from the past, humans and birds alike simply will not do or say them. How does this happen?

Behaviors that no longer serve a purpose become obsolete and are replaced by behaviors that have a purpose in the current environment. Unused old behaviors are replaced by useful new behaviors, but changing any habitual behavior isn't usually easy.

In helping a bird to discontinue an established, habitual use of profanity, begin by evaluating when the profanity appears. Is it during play or during the regular practice of the bird's vocabulary? Does it occur at a particular time of day or when events in the home stimulate it as a response? If you know when a

*Tight feathers, elongated neck, and round eyes are typical in a grey that is nervous or frightened.*

sound is usually made, you are well on your way to replacing that sound with a different one.

## Human Body Sounds

Other nuisance sounds African greys are especially fond of include burps and belches and other gastronomic body expressions. Guiding a grey parrot away from human body sounds is often more difficult than guiding it away from profanity, as few spoken words resemble these sounds. Again, we must anticipate the behavior before it occurs and distract the bird to different behavior. The bird must be distracted to sounds that are both more acceptable to humans and that are just as fun for the bird to make. Laughter is this type of self-rewarding activity. It's usually easy to distract an interested, well-motivated bird to laughter before the gross body sounds begin. Again, if you've been unable to divert away from an unwanted sound, be sure not to laugh after they begin.

## Other Bird and Animal Sounds

It's amazing how many apartment managers who, when told that I have birds, have asked me, "Do they bark?"

Sounds acquired from other animals are among the most annoying vocalizations observed in grey parrots. Acquired animal sounds are, like human body sounds and electronic sounds, usually more difficult to modify than human words; however, they are also sometimes more predictably enacted at a particular time of day. A companion grey parrot might do hen cockatiel at sunrise or Blue-crowned Amazon when it's time to eat.

To divert from these behaviors, the daily routine must be changed in some substantial way so that enactment of the behavior is avoided. The grey parrot that does hen cockatiel at sunrise might have to have a more lightproof cover so that it doesn't know when the sun rises. Then the breakfast routine can be changed in some way to create an entirely different interactive ritual, perhaps by removing the bird to a perch to eat breakfast rather than providing the morning meal in the cage.

## Stimulation

As in humans, a grey parrot that finds joy in only a few things is likely to become obsessed with those few things. This is one more example of how lack of stimulation creates bad behavior in companion birds. That famous old source of almost all bird behavior problems, boredom, also contributes to habitually redundant behaviors including the repeating of nuisance words and sounds.

Here we can expand the bird's experiences so that it learns new ways to enjoy life. If the bird is encouraged to do many different, diverse behaviors, it will spend less time repeating nuisance sounds and the offensive words and sounds will gradually disappear.

# Cautiousness, Fearfulness, and Phobic Behavior

An individual grey's personality is a combination of learned and inherited characteristics. In captivity, the bird has no predators, but rather, may exhibit an inherited tendency to respond with fear to many situations. Even boredom can lead to induced or enhanced fear reactions in a grey parrot. Accidental reinforcement can cause cautiousness to progress to shyness, fearfulness, panic, or even phobic behaviors.

## The Purpose of Fear

Caution is important in the life of a wild grey parrot. Greys can be seen circling a clearing before they land[1] as they are prey species that must be always watchful for those who would make dinner of them. Because of how easily most African parrots turn to the fight-or-flight response, it's easy to surmise that these birds are probably more subject to predation in the wild than their New World or Pacific species relatives.

In captivity, fear response contributes to behavioral problems such as biting—the "fight" part of a well-developed fight-or-flight response—thrashing, falling, inability to regrow repeatedly knocked-out wing feathers, and even (commonly) feather shredding or snapping or (rarely) feather plucking. Shyness, fearfulness, and phobic behavior rather than aggression often accompany self-induced feather damage—shredding, snapping, or plucking—in grey parrots. Additionally, an experienced avian behavior consultant will usually admit the response to treatments for aggression is generally more predictable than responses to treatments for fearfulness.

Within the African grey parrots, the Timneh appears to be more resistant to the development of truly phobic responses than the Red-tailed greys. A companion Timneh grey is not as easily provoked to the fight-or-flight response as a companion Red-tailed grey. However, both fear biting and thrashing can be seen in both species.

## When Cautiousness Leads to Phobias

We know that repeated enactment of the fight-or-flight response by a grey parrot, or sometimes even one severe incidence of the fight-or-flight response induced by panic can stimulate ongoing, constant panic behaviors whenever humans are present. We have likened this condition to phobic mental illness, but we are not altogether sure that this condition doesn't serve some unknown purpose. Sometimes, despite the best intentions, the hardest work, and the kindest handling, a grey parrot inexplicably falls into this behavior. If this behavior were completely maladaptive, we believe it would not appear in these birds. There must be some adaptive aspect for the wild grey. "Under normal circumstances stress responses are beneficial and permit the animal to react more competently to an emergency. However, when the stressful challenge is prolonged, the responses become maladaptive, leading to decreased resistance to disease and abnormal behavior."[2]

Wild greys are cautious by nature. In the home, cautiousness can be seen as a tendency toward shyness. While a fear response can be direct and immediate, a grey parrot doesn't always respond immediately to a situation. The grey likes to sit back and assess a situation, often drawing clues from others—humans, birds, and so on) to determine the appropriate response. New toys and new people may have to wait through an assessment period, which varies in length depending on the bird, before the parrot is ready for interaction.

After assessing a situation, the grey might decide it is scary and respond with fear. The most extreme form of fear is panic, which involves growling and thrashing. Humans who are watching the bird with wide eyes to see how it will respond are exhibiting body language that signals caution or fear to the bird, while some greys that know their owners might understand that this isn't really what the human means. Many greys see their human as having the cautious pose a grey would take if it perceived danger. No matter how the bird reaches the decision, fear is a response to an object or situation that has been determined to be a threat.

When a grey's fear is generalized and the bird panics in many situations, it is sometimes labeled phobic. A phobic bird exhibits unreasonable fear. It will broadly generalize what situations should be feared, so that humans may no longer be able to identify exactly what the bird fears.

Many greys are afraid of people's hands or eyes. Manipulating a parrot's perception of appearance, such as by hiding hands or by allowing the bird to see only one eye at a time, as it would see another bird, can sometimes generate more appropriate responses. Diet can also contribute to hypersensitivity similar to phobic behaviors.

## Problematic Fear Responses

African greys are born altricial, that is, they must depend upon their parents—natural or human—to supply every need in order to survive. During the months parents have control, a young grey parrot must be given all the information required to live on its own. At a certain point, the bird must be ready to become physically and emotionally independent.

When a grey reaches the state where it should become independent and is either lacking the tools to function independently or perceives that a human or humans have too much control, the parrot experiences stress. At this point the bird should be able to make food choices and meet its own nutritional needs. It should be able to climb and hold onto perches. Nails should

have points that are sharp enough to grip, and perches shouldn't be too large in diameter. The bird's wings must be long enough to control falls. The bird must be able to entertain itself when nobody else is around. It must be able to call to "flock members" and to feel like part of a flock. Problematic fear responses may appear when the bird is forced to be independent before it is ready or when it is not given enough independence when it *is* ready.

A hand-fed grey's experiences with its surrogate human parents will color its view of relationships with people. The "parent" is trusted to help the baby parrot learn the tools needed to function. If the job is handed off to another person, the bird's sense of security can be seriously undermined. Weaning the baby onto solid food in preparation for life in captivity is best completed by the same parent or set of parents.

## Fear Relating to Wings and Nails

Improper grooming, especially improperly trimmed wing feathers, can contribute to fearfulness in African grey parrots. A parrot uses its wings, toenails, and beak in basic locomotion. If any of these are rendered useless, the bird is in danger of falling. Uncontrolled falling can establish fear of falling. This leads the bird to fear climbing and to fear stepping onto surfaces, such as a hand, that might then be fallen from. Since the only escape mechanism has been removed, the bird might actually become afraid of being afraid. This is when true phobia sets in, and the bird will begin to panic in more and more circumstances. Eventually almost anything sends the bird thrashing and growling to the floor of the cage.

A young grey's wings should be trimmed only enough to keep it from crashing into the window or from gaining enough speed to injure itself. The bird should be nearly able to fly. Secondary feathers should never be cut since these are the feathers that provide control in landing. Like the inside flaps on an airplane's wings, the secondary flight feathers are the "brakes," and a bird cannot stop gracefully and confidently without them. There should always be enough of the primary feathers left to protect the new primary feathers growing in.

Blood feathers on a grey are very sensitive, especially on the wings, particularly if the feathers are trimmed short (see discussion on page 86). A bird with new primaries growing in may become very protective of its wings. It might avoid flapping and any situations that might stimulate flapping. If a bird is feeling especially protective of its wings, if it senses any "danger," it might resist coming out of the cage. Many parrot owners, having been bullied by other types of parrots by not taking enough control, will try to force the bird to come out of the cage, whether it wants to or not. A grey parrot might balk at having the issue pushed. A typical scenario is that the bird falls to the bottom of the cage, breaking the feather it was protecting. Now the bird is holding a grudge against the owner for causing the fall so that it might panic and automatically jump or thrash the next time it sees the owner, and a cycle of fearfulness begins.

The grey parrot's sensitive temperament is best served with very noninvasive grooming configuration and technique. Consider the possibility that a bird outgrowing a fearful phase might regain self-assurance exactly as those old, cut wing feathers are replaced with full new ones. A grey parrot with a tendency to be overly cautious may require full wing feathers in order to retain confidence. Both phobic behaviors and feather-damaging disorders of all types are probably more common in grey parrots with trimmed wing feathers. These individuals should be allowed to keep full wings.

The Red-tailed grey and, to a lesser extent, the Timneh grey can have a tendency to knock new wing feathers out as they regrow. If a bird is having trouble regrowing wing feathers, be sure to provide smaller than usual, easily gripped perches to prevent falling and thrashing. Limit the number of toys, but provide multiple chewable branches to climb and exercise both wings and beaks on. Sometimes trimming off the open part of the feather as the new feather is growing in will make the feather less likely to be knocked out, but be sure not to cut into the membrane providing blood supply.

*Natural branches with bark provide a surface that is easy to grip.*

## Manipulating the Bird's Environment

The environment can either provide a sense of security or destroy it. For example, noisy species such as Hyacinth macaws may upset shyer birds that perceive that the macaws' frequent vocalizations indicate the constant presence of danger.

Obviously, the feeling of being in constant danger can harm a bird's health and disposition. We could address the problem of noisy birds by housing species separately, but we may be able to build in a sense of safety with other environmental elements. Manipulating height, housing the bird either higher or lower, for example, can enhance a grey parrot's sense of security, as can the addition of hiding opportunities, which might include a little tent (a hide box), a towel over one-third of the cage, restricted sight of other birds, or moving the cage to a more sheltered location, perhaps across the room from traffic areas. Don't forget that the towel game is sometimes helpful in these situations.

## Messages from Humans

Sometimes, the stimulus for a bird's panic response comes from human caregivers. If a bird has developed a fear of fast-moving hands, or if hands it knows well change in appearance, such as hands with newly manicured nails, the bird might respond with panic. Hold your hands out of sight in your pockets or behind your back until calm behavior can be stimulated, patterned, and reinforced Also, expect reactions to changes in your hair color, haircut, or when you wear a hat.

A grey parrot that has been previously panicked by severe eye contact might thrash, bite, or flee any human eye contact. This can be distressing when feeding the bird or changing the substrata in the cage. If it is possible without provoking panic, remove the bird when servicing the cage. Try avoiding eye contact if you must service the cage with the bird inside. A bird can be slowly guided out of this behavior by use of the games and nonthreatening interactions described on page 121.

## Guide to Games

Some grey parrots that do not tolerate physical contact simply prefer to interact in other ways. These various interactions include eye games, body language games, and other interactive games that involve no physical contact. Especially in the

*Some greys may experience stress when kept in close proximity to larger, noisier species.*

case of shy grey parrots, it's a real advantage to know how to connect emotionally without actual touching the bird.

**1.** Some birds react fearfully to hands and eyes. If this is the case, hide your hands and look at a cautious or unfamiliar bird with one eye at a time. This eye should be squinting and not wide open.

**2.** Any eye contact may be threatening to a shy bird, so don't maintain eye contact, or squint your eyes until they are nearly shut. Gradually open them as the bird becomes comfortable looking at you and letting you look back.

**3.** Remain absolutely motionless until the bird moves. Many grey parrots "freeze" (remain motionless) when they see a stranger. If you copy this behavior, the bird is more likely to recognize you as behaviorally similar, and therefore, probably a safe flock member.

**4.** Stoop over so that your entire head is lower than the bird's body. Because of the desire to achieve the highest status in the flock, many birds gain natural confidence by being allowed to be higher than humans. Almost any parrot will find a human who is sitting on the floor absolutely baffling and will often come down to see what on earth that human is doing there.

**5.** Play the blinking game. A frightened animal will not blink while maintaining eye contact. Demonstrate that you are not afraid by blinking while maintaining eye contact from a distance. An interested, interactive parrot will close its eyes or blink back to show that it is not afraid.

**6.** Play "Peek-a-boo" around any interesting corner, reading materials, towels, or clothing—not your hands, as a shy grey parrot may be sensitive to hands.

**7.** Mimic the bird's friendly body language. When you see the bird stretch a greeting by extending one or both wings (mantling), try to show the bird that you feel the same way it feels by exhibiting the same body language.

**8.** Mimic simple sounds from across the room or around a corner including tapping or knocking when you hear the bird tap or knock. If your bird plays with a bell and rings the bell, try ringing a bell in response. Try to entice the bird to respond to your response.

**9.** Share food with the bird. If the bird is cautious and has never taken food from you before, it might throw the food or drop it. The bird can often be persuaded to take the food by manipulating the window of opportunity during which the food is offered. This is also called "Keep Away," see page 121). Offer the food for a few seconds, then drop it or take it away. Wait a few seconds, then offer the food again, dropping it or taking it away before the bird can take it. Also, giving the food to a rival increases the effectiveness of this game.

**10.** Play drop-the-toy-and-pick-it-up. This is probably the game most frequently initiated by parrots with humans. It's the bird equivalent of "fetch," only the human does the fetching. The bird drops the toy or the spoon or the grape; the human picks it up and hands it to the bird. The bird flashes its eyes, puts beak to toy, then suddenly drops the toy again. The human picks it up.

**11.** "I'll wear toys for you." Arrange to have old glasses, small wooden or plastic toys, or bird-safe jewelry that the bird can steal. Play with your toys, or have someone else play with your toys, and allow the bird to steal them.

**12.** Demonstrate the joys of touching with other humans, pets, or birds. Find a cooperative friend who enjoys being hugged and touched and petted, and demonstrate the joys of hugging, touching, and petting for the bird. This game resembles the model/rival method of speech training in that it often stimulates the bird to compete for human attention.

**Note:** A grey's eyes will be almond-shaped or almost squinty when it is calm and relaxed, while a human has a tendency to round the eyes when feeling compassionate or concerned. A grey can translate this as nervousness or fear and it may become afraid as well. This often happens when the person is introducing something new to a grey or is being introduced to a new grey. Many greys learn that this is not the correct interpretation for the look humans give. Still, to convey calmness and confidence to a grey it is best to slightly squint your eyes. It's

even better to include moving the head forward and slightly lower to mimic the posture that draws many people to conclude that greys look like vultures.

# Reacting to Humans

Sometimes a bird that is going through even an enduring fearful stage will meet a human to whom it is naturally, inexorably drawn. This can come like a thunderbolt, like love at first sight. Curiously, in greys, this is not always a situation of "overbonding," in which after falling for a particular human, the bird remains fearful or aggressive with other humans. We have seen grey parrots that were previously panicked by interactions with any human learn to accept humans after meeting only one human it naturally connected with.

Sometimes a bird will encounter someone it considers a rival or a threat, or it will suddenly decide that it is terrified of someone who has not done anything to deserve such treatment. The bird can be gently guided away from these feelings. Start with games and nonthreatening interactions (see page 121). Use the disfavored person's name in tandem with the bird's: *"Jaco's Uncle Charlie"* or *"Uncle Charlie's Jaco"* when guiding the bird to include the person in its group of accepted associates. Then progress to the towel game, step-ups, and outings.

Greys do not like to change their minds and pushing them to do so is often rewarded with resentment. An insecure grey may actually use hating someone as a way to build confidence. Many greys will stop reacting negatively to a person when that negative behavior no longer serves a purpose, and waiting for the bird to change its mind is sometimes the best recourse. Slipping treats to the bird in the meantime is often a good idea, as is showering affection on another pet or rival in front of the parrot so it sees what it is missing. Attention paid to the bird's favorite person is almost always perceived in an unfavorable light.

As mentioned, greys like to whistle and can often be persuaded to strike up a relationship with someone who provides them with tantalizing vocal entertainment. The whistling distracts them from being afraid and provides them with a sense of communicating with the flock. This interaction can help foster a sense of security and should be included in the daily interactions with a grey, whether it shows signs of being fearful or not.

# Outings

Sometimes new and better bonds can be forged by outings into unfamiliar territory, especially outings with less favored humans. The bird might feel better connected to the person because of insecurity in unfamiliar locations. Improved bonding can result, especially if there is an opportunity for a "rescue scenario" (see below), but sometimes just taking the bird for a ride in the car will generate noticeable improvements.

## The Rescue Scenario

Sometimes, better bonds can be forged between a parrot and a human it doesn't like by taking outings together. It probably works something like this:

Did you ever walk into a social gathering and know absolutely no one in the room, and then, after an hour of lingering by the punch bowl, feeling awkward and out of place and talking to no one, across the room you see someone you know only slightly. This is someone you might not have particularly liked before or have been lukewarm to at best, but suddenly, that person looks really safe and familiar and reminds you of home.

Then, out of nowhere comes the most annoying stranger you have ever seen walking straight up to you and putting a hand on your forearm. You withdraw and turn to go, but the annoying person follows you through the crowd. Suddenly, the person you know, the one you didn't like before, steps between you and the awful stranger.

"Back off," that now lovely person says to the awful stranger, taking your arm and leading you to a quiet foyer. A better bond is forged; that relationship is changed forever, regardless of the setting.

In the same way, if the less favored person is the only person the bird knows in a strange place, the bird will be very nice to that person at that time in that location. This sets up a pattern for the bird to also be nice in other places at other times. This works especially well if it can involve a rescue scenario, as in *Androcles and the Lion.*

# Behavioral Intervention

The grey parrot's extreme intelligence renders it more behaviorally sensitive than many other parrots. A grey can easily learn or improvise a very impressive array of diverse unwanted behaviors.

If humans are being repeatedly outsmarted by a cantankerous grey parrot or baffled by a totally terrified bird, professional intervention might make a huge difference. A bird that cannot be touched by anyone familiar will often prove perfectly cooperative with a professional stranger. Owners may be stunned or moved to tears, and comment that they don't recognize that precious creature—with just a tiny remnant of yesterday's blood on the tip of its beak.

If you need help, seek a parrot behavior consultant who can document experience with grey parrots. Professionals in this relatively new field can be the first line of defense against the accumulation of troubling behaviors. Potential problems that might require professional assistance in the grey parrot include those we have discussed: fearfulness, biting, diving, behavioral feather chewing, and annoying vocalizations.

The words "behavioral consultant" or "behaviorist" are important here, for an effective behavioral counselor probably works more like a golf or tennis coach than a psychiatrist. A behavioral consultant should be more focused on how to change the bird's behavior than on judging how the bird's behavior came to be that way. A good behaviorist will deal compassionately with the bird and compassionately with the owner.

In order to change the bird's behavior, one must have an understanding of the forces that stimulated and reinforced the behavior into patterns. In this way, distractions and more pleasing patterns can be planned for, stimulated and reinforced. Most behaviorists will prefer to do an in-home consultation and will probably take a history in order to plan strategies for changing the bird's behavior.

Your favorite breeder, bird store, or avian veterinarian should be able to refer you to a parrot behavior consultant in your area. They might recommend telephone counseling. There are quite a few behavioral alternatives in the consultant ads in the back of your favorite bird magazine and on the Internet. Some are wonderful; some are awful. Look for places where kindness and open minds prevail. Ask for references from others who have actually consulted with a particular behaviorist about a similar problem in a grey parrot.

## What to Expect

**1.** Expect an initial screening consultation by telephone. Before making an appointment, many behavior consultants will spend a few minutes on the phone asking the age, source, type of bird, nature, and duration of the problem. You may then expect a description of what kind of expenditure of time and money might be needed in order to correct the problem. A professional will also be evaluating your responses and trying to determine whether or not the two of you have a rapport. Expect to be referred to a different consultant if either of you don't feel a good emotional connection.

**2.** The consultant might offer group, telephone, or in-home counseling, depending upon your location and the nature of the problem. Group work must be done very carefully for reasons of health and safety of the bird. Telephone counseling is attractive for simple problems of short duration, but in-home evaluations remain the most dependable way to solve long-term, enduring problems.

**3.** The behavior consultant will be looking for things such as diet, housing, and handling elements that might be contributing to the bird's behavior. He or she will be looking for indications of typical interactions between the bird and other family

*For the best results, seek professional help as soon as behavior problems occur.*

members, as well as making observations about how the bird is responding to this unfamiliar person in the home.

**4.** A thorough behavioral evaluation will probably include grooming or toweling the bird in order to observe its responses. The behaviorist may make recommendations regarding the bird's responses to the towel.

**5.** If the bird is shy, the behavior consultant might not even touch the bird, as invasive handling can worsen such conditions. In cases involving shyness or fearfulness, expect the behaviorist to offer suggestions regarding adjusting the bird's behavior through making changes in the environment. This response to the bird's behavioral needs is often the easiest, most obvious, and most effective way to change bird behavior. Some environmental manipulations might worsen or reinforce the unwanted behaviors, so sometimes the environmental elements are manipulated in various ways to study the ways the bird responds to the changes.

**6.** The behavioral consultant might want to observe feather condition and the bird's responses to showering. The easiest way to do this, of course, is to give the bird a bath as a part of the behavioral evaluation.

**7.** Expect the possibility of a veterinarian referral and expect a responsible companion bird behavior consultant to refer you to an appropriate avian veterinarian if there is suspicion that health issues may factor into the case.

**8.** Expect the behavior consultant to seem to be favoring the welfare of the bird over human interests. As an advocate for the bird, a behavior consultant must be ever-vigilant, as many subtle human interactions may prove dangerous to a bird in the care of those humans. Whether a situation of danger to the bird from other pets, rambunctious children, spousal abuse, drug or alcohol abuse, or simply danger from Teflon cookware and excessive forgetfulness, a caring bird behavior consultant will try to confront the problem, sometimes by referring to human behavioral and psychological counseling. The relationship between the family and the bird behavior consultant should be friendly and interactive. Expect a professional bird behavior consultant to keep your case confidential unless he or she has asked permission to write about the case, which can be done in a way to protect your privacy.

**9.** Expect to be offered more than one option for the modification of a particular behavioral problem. Every companion bird environment is different, and you are the most significant element of the bird's environment. Some humans can more readily understand and implement one type of plan than another; therefore, any bird behavior consultant worth his or her salt should be able to suggest more than one approach to the modification of a particular behavior. An effective communicator should be able to explain the same approach in more than one way so that all parties—even young children—can understand and implement a behavioral intervention program.

**10.** Expect to be required to reinforce appropriate new behaviors, for it is the training of humans that produces enduring changes in the bird. Expect to see new behaviors; whenever one behavior is modified, new behaviors arise. For example, when treating shyness or feather chewing, especially feather chewing related to shyness in the grey parrot, we would expect to see some aggression develop. Be prepared to make further changes when new behaviors appear to take the place of the old behaviors.

**11.** Expect to enjoy the interaction and to have your life touched in a

*A well-adjusted bird will eat any place or time.*

significant way. It's not unusual for family members to weep with joy when they make a major breakthrough in the rehabilitation of a troubling parrot behavior problem. It is important to like and to trust the professionals who work with your bird; your life and your bird's life may be changed from this day on.

We can't teach a bird to forget a behavior. We can teach the bird behaviors to replace the ones we don't want. Also, behavior doesn't immediately change permanently. That is, it comes and goes. A behavior that is being eliminated will not suddenly stop. It will stop, in response to behavioral manipulation, then reappear, then stop, then reappear. If the behavioral intervention is working properly, each reappearance of the unwanted behavior will be of shorter duration and less intensity. There will be more tail wags and other happiness behaviors, more enactments of behaviors being reinforced, and the unwanted behavior will gradually disappear.

[1] Parrot's: Look Who's Talking, Video.

[2] Greg J. Harrison and Linda R. Harrison, B.S., *Clinical Avian Medicine and Surgery*. W. B. Saunders Company, 1986, p. 601.

## Chapter Eight

# Feathers and Feather Problems

Few behavior problems are more troubling than the self-destruction of feathers by the bird. Self-inflicted feather damage, here called "feather picking," is a complex problem, and many factors are involved. Appropriate patterning, a cage that is neither too large nor too small, careful positioning of the cage, gentle handling, full-spectrum lighting, and appropriate diet are only a few elements necessary for a happy, independent parrot. The bird must have satisfactory relationships with humans, objects, and locations. It must have an understanding of time and be conditioned to accept changes. The bird learns self-rewarding or independent play habits. The bird must learn that it will not be abandoned, that when people go away, they always come back.

Field biologist David Manry tells us that when a wild animal is confronted with a situation that it does not have a corresponding instinctual behavior for, it may choose another behavior rather than doing nothing at all. The animal can become obsessive about this inappropriate behavior and perform it to extremes.

Almost any behavior in the animal's repertoire can be used as a "displacement behavior," including preening, pulling feathers, or even chewing feathers, nails, or skin. There are many situations in captive life that African grey parrots do not have instinctual behaviors for.

## Molting and Other Explainable Feather Loss

Some new bird owners may be concerned that their baby grey parrots are "secretly plucking tail feathers" because feathers are found on the floor or cage bottom. There is usually no cause for concern if these are individual feathers or feathers in pairs, as this is part of molting, the natural process of replacing feathers. During warm weather, a bird will lose and regrow feathers in a symmetrical configuration along the lines of circulation known as feather tracts. Wing feathers are molted out and regrown in mirror image, a configuration that would not, in the wild, inhibit flight ability. If the flight feathers are not regrowing symmetrically, this could be an indication that feathers were damaged or knocked out and had already regrown or that the bird had removed some of them.

Feather loss or damage can also be caused by other birds. Chewed feathers on places where the bird cannot reach, such as the cheeks, head, or nape, are an indication that the bird is being chewed by another bird, and that they should be separated.

Happy, exuberant juveniles are also known to damage feathers during active play. Baby African parrots commonly have bent or dirty tail feathers. A few tail feathers might break, but most of them should last until nearly molting time (one year old). If multiple feathers of the second tail break, it is often due to a nutritional deficiency. Baby greys that have not experienced their first molt are also known to occasionally chew off dirty or damaged feathers. This is also not usually cause for concern and will probably not be ongoing.

If all of a grey parrot's wing or tail feathers suddenly wind up on the floor of the cage, it may be due to a traumatic incident. African grey parrots are extremely sensitive and are occasionally subject to being frightened in the dark and suffer reactions similar to night frights in cockatiels. This can result in the loss of all tail

*Obvious bare spots may indicate feather picking.*

feathers, and occasionally in the loss of wing feathers. Although tail feathers can be extremely loose, especially in hot weather, the wing feathers are connected to the cuticle of the bone and are intended to stay in place and function even under the most arduous circumstances. Efforts must be made to protect the bird from being frightened into self-injury. Look for mice or other animals moving around in the dark.

# Other Feather Problems

### Feather Chewing, Shredding, or Fringing

Feather chewing or shredding begins with damage to the edge of the barbs of the contour feathers, sometimes giving the feathers a notched, fringed, or hairlike appearance. Both mild and progressive feather shredding behaviors can sometimes exist for years before anyone notices them. The first sign of this type of feather damage is often visible as individual "fibers" or remnants of the barbs seen floating on the surface of the water dish or on the papers in the bottom of the cage. This form of feather damage is often referred to as "overpreening" or inappropriate preening. If the bird thinks that the owner is the only "fun toy," it will not play with other toys and will not develop independent play behaviors. It will instead, usually sit around preening in anticipation of that treasured interaction with the favorite human (see section on toys and independent play, page 24).

### Feather Snapping

Feather snapping, a more acute, quickly progressing form of feather damage, is not uncommon in grey parrots. Snapping involves breaking the shaft of the feather. This can begin in a small way when a bird snaps off the rachis or central feather shaft near the outer end of the feather resulting in feathers ending in a V shape. In a more acute phase, this might involve snapping the feather off at the base, leaving no contour feather visible outside the down. The bird might snip the contour feather and down feathers off, leaving bare patches of skin showing. Often, wing and tail feathers are targeted.

This is the most sudden-appearing form of feather damage, when a bird is apparently in full feather one minute and there's a naked bird with a pile of feathers under the perch a half-hour later. Feather snapping does not injure the skin, and there is no danger of skin infection as when a feather is pulled from the follicle.

### Feather Plucking or Pulling

True feather plucking involves pulling the entire feather out of the follicle. Any feather can be targeted. The bird might pull feathers with the beak or feet. A parrot might target fully formed feathers or feathers that still have blood supply. These behaviors can put the parrot at risk for skin infections.

Feather pulling is especially common around the vent or around the uropygial (preening) gland, as well as around the neck where dirty feathers might be especially annoying to a bird. Pulling or chewing off dirty feathers is common behavior in baby parrots that have not yet experienced their first molt. It might be ongoing, or it might be a simple temporary response to dirty or damaged feathers.

If there are no health issues, occasional feather pulling, especially by juveniles, often resolves spontaneously with the first molt, and is no cause for concern. However, a juvenile pulling, snapping, or chewing off dirty or damaged feathers should be bathed more often (see showering, page 135), exercised more, monitored carefully, and carefully not reinforced to pull feathers.

Ongoing feather pulling in adult greys, more than any other form of self-inflicted feather damage, is suspected to have an organic origin. If there is no identifiable illness, we must suspect food, fumes, or allergies when this behavior appears.

### Self-mutilation

While feather damage is often mild and not an outright threat to the bird's health, self-inflicted damage to skin requires immediate professional intervention. The self destruction of skin, the skin on the feet, or even toes can be related to poor diet, to inhaled environmental toxins, including nicotine, or to poor perches. Nicotine can be absorbed from human skin through the skin on the bottom of the bird's feet. Cigarettes, especially, must be absolutely eliminated to avoid the danger of progressive damage.

# First Signs

The most common places for parrots to start picking feathers are the upper legs or thighs, feathers around the neck in a necklace pattern, the sides of the chest just over the thighs, or the tops of the wings going down the back. This will be evident by the appearance of patches of damaged feathers, patches of gray down poking out through the smooth contour feathers, or bald spots. Birds chewing on new feathers will often leave the evidence as feather particles in the water dish, and bald spots will be slow to appear. Greys will sometimes snap off wing feathers. This might seem like normal molting of the flight feathers unless the owner carefully inspects them to make sure the follicle end of the feather is present. Sometimes the first sign even a very astute owner notices is a completely bald bird with a large pile of feathers in the bottom of the cage. The owner will have had no warning that such an event was coming.

The most common time for feather picking to appear in African greys is November through February. Whether this is a result of seasonal hormonal cycles, indoor winter

*Feather picking might start around the neck.*

air quality, lack of humidity, or a response to artificial heat is unknown, but each of these elements might play a part.

# Possible Causes

## Stress Reactions

Because self-induced feather damage is considered to be a reaction to stress, you must look, first of all, when this syndrome appears, for illness or physical problems. See an avian veterinarian at the first sign of unexplainable feather damage. Don't wait; go quickly, before the behavior becomes habitual. It's all right to ask about potential illness, zinc and cal-

cium levels, yeast, and giardia (see below). Be prepared to hear your local veterinarian's experience with contributing health-related issues in your specific geographic area. Sometimes, the veterinarian will find no health-related issues and will suggest diet or habitat manipulation and/or behavioral counseling.

## Physiological Causes

Certain disease states are notorious for bringing on bouts of feather-damaging behavior. Many cases of feather mutilation can be linked to a cause detectable by a veterinarian. For this reason, the first step in combating such an incident is a complete veterinary workup. Disease states in parrots are generally a reflection of stress that may be physical or emotional, real or imagined. So, while the veterinarian may find a physical cause related to the self-destructive behavior, presumably this is not the sole cause of the plucking, and the plucking and the disease may be caused by stress. When possible, it is preferable that a holistic approach be taken with self-mutilating birds. There is almost always much more to treat than a disease.

Aspergilosis, giardia, and staph infections are commonly associated with feather picking. These are generally considered "opportunistic" organisms, invading a body whose immune system is impaired or otherwise compromised. Thyroid conditions are also commonly diagnosed. Thyroid malfunction is difficult to diagnose positively, and treating minor thyroid problems medically can increase the bird's stress and cause even more mutilation problems.

Health problems must be eradicated before fully focusing on emotional issues. In many places where there are no veterinarians available who have experience with birds, doctors may be worried about missing a medical condition and therefore will prescribe medication "just in case." While their intentions are good and this treatment plan might work under other circumstances, feather pickers should not be treated in this manner. The simple act of treating them can increase stress, making the problem worse, and there is always a risk that medication can harm or inhibit normal body functions.

Some veterinarians may wish to treat self-induced feather damage with such drugs as Valium, Haldoperidol, or Prozac. Although medical treatment is absolutely necessary when illness or other uncomfortable health conditions exist, benefits from the use of tranquilizers or other mood enhancers is as yet unproven. These treatments should be considered a temporary, last resort sort of thing after all efforts have been made to resolve the problem with behavioral or environmental techniques.

Holistic approaches can often correct problems less invasively and address some other contributing aspects. Contact allergies can be implicated in many cases of plucking associated with the legs in particular. Smokers carry elements of tobacco on their fingers. Some birds can be sensitive to certain types of wood used in perches or to the bacteria that can grow on them. Parrots can be sensitive to foods or to the artificial ingredients some foods contain. Artificial colors and preservatives are best avoided. Parrots can also have allergies to airborne particles and suffer something akin to hay fever in humans.

## Dry Skin or External Parasites

Some grey parrots might pick at themselves in a way that would suggest they had a sudden extreme itch or bug crawling on them. The bird's skin might appear dry with flakes of dead skin on it. It is tempting to think that the bird has dry skin or mites and to want to spray it with something to solve the problem, but again, this is not usually a situation to treat. Parrot skin often has a dry appearance to it, and in many of the places where parrots are kept as pets, there are no mites around that could infect the bird.

A parrot should not have dry skin. Humans will often have dry skin and will treat their own dry skin with lotions, but human dry skin comes from subjecting the skin to harsh chemicals and sun, and not taking in proper nutrition including water, and taking in too much salt and caffeine or alcohol. Parrots, hopefully, do not have these problems. If a grey's skin is actually dry, the reason for this should be addressed rather than trying to treat it topically. A rain forest bird that now lives in the desert may need a humidifier and frequent showers to keep the skin sufficiently hydrated. Proper diet is also necessary for good skin.

### Diet

Like humans, parrots have a better attitude and outlook when they have been eating well. A poor or inadequate diet stresses not only the body, but the psyche as well. Fresh foods are very important in a bird's diet. A variety of organic produce would be most desirable as birds can react to coatings and pesticides. The mixes suggested by Alicia McWatters, Ph.D., or in *Psittacine Aviculture* by Richard Schubott at ABRC, are excellent bases for a balanced diet of fresh foods.

Birds are often less finicky when fed pellets and fresh food instead of seed as the base diet. Pellets are also the easiest way for most bird keepers to provide a nutritious diet (see page 80). Preferably, the pellets should have no preservatives or artificial colors and a large number of food ingredients. Water should be clean and clear without vitamins or other additives. Anything added to the water can accumulate on the beak and can be deposited on the feathers while preening. Some parrots develop feather-picking habits because they do not have access to clear water.

Food sensitivities might be contributing to feather pulling, so manipulation of the bird's diet can help.

Sometimes eliminating salt or oil and, in African greys more than other parrots, improving calcium sources and absorption can sometimes help. Occasionally, radical evaluation of the diet must be made, possibly removing all but one food from the diet and then gradually adding foods to observe their effect on the bird.

# Dealing with Feather Picking

### Exercise and Showers

The entire makeup of an African grey, every bone and metabolic process, lends itself to explosive expenditures of energy. This is not an exclusively metabolic and physical process, but rather, also fills emotional needs. Few of our captive feathered friends are getting the exercise they really need. This has repercussions on their overall physical health, attitude, and stress levels.

**Flapping exercises:** Placing the bird on a play area does no more to ensure adequate exercise than dropping a devoted couch potato off at the gym. Both will most probably spend most of the time standing around. Humans must encourage the bird to work off excess energy through flapping exercises, which are best done over a bed or soft carpeted floor in case the bird should fall. Lowering the hand the bird is standing on or rolling it back and forth can encourage the bird to flap.

Some parrots will attempt to stop the procedure by grabbing the hand with the beak. A hand-held perch can be slowly rolled in the same manner. A grey parrot needs to flap every day until it is breathing very deeply, probably with its beak open.

**Showering:** Likewise, regular showering can resolve several stresses associated with feather mutilation, such as lack of adequate humidity and soiled feathers. Showering uses excess energy that can turn into frustration and is refreshing to the bird. A showered bird also uses its preening energy more evenly over its whole body. An unshowered bird would be more likely to preen problem spots such as the sides of the chest or over the back, leading to ragged and over-preened feathers.

**Spraying:** Parrots have taste buds on the roof of the mouth and no saliva on their tongues. Spraying a bad-tasting substance on the feathers often has no effect. Many times, the substance sprayed will be viewed as dirt, and the parrot will preen even harder. Occasionally, a bird will stop picking if the owner is diligent about spraying the bitter substance; however, birds will often have the same good results if the owner diligently sprays clear water.

## The Cage

The cage should be designed in a way that is useful to the bird and placed in an appropriate area (see page 67). Some birds prefer to be able to see what is going on while still being out of the way of the actual action. It is rarely a good idea to put a feather picker out of the way where no one will bother it. This will often increase a sense of separation from the flock and increase anxiety. Raising or lowering the cage will almost always affect the grey's sense of security, some doing better when lowered, others preferring to be higher up. Some birds will stop picking on their feathers when relocated to a more secure and smaller cage. Other birds will start picking if they feel too pent up in a small cage.

## Lighting

There are three types of cones or light-detecting cells in our eyes. These structures provide us with visual interpretation of color. One type of cone detects blue light, one red, and one green. Birds have four types of cones for visual interpretation of color, and the wavelengths of light they are sensitive to are shifted to the left of the spectrum.[1] They do not pick up as much information from the red end of the spectrum as we do; however, they pick up more information from the violet and ultra-violet ends of the spectrum. Since we cannot see it, we have no idea what things reflect light in this end of the spectrum.

Lighting that is labeled "full-spectrum" may be a full-spectrum light as perceived by humans, or may be a full-spectrum light as perceived by birds. A full-spectrum light serving birds would emit wavelengths in the part of the spectrum parrots can

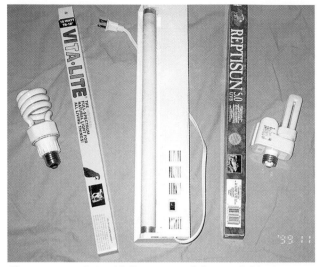

*There are a variety of full spectrum lights available that would be beneficial to a parrot.*

reducer. African greys are from equatorial regions of Africa where there is little seasonal change in day length. These parrots need 10 to 12 hours of sleep at night year-round. Daytime naps do not make up for lost sleep at night. Sometimes this means making use of a sleep cage—a small cage in a separate room—so the bird is not disturbed by late night television or visitors

## Entertainment

Boredom is a major contributor to feather mutilating. Life in captivity is never going to be as exciting as life in the wild, and we probably don't want it to be. Giving the bird appropriate toys and encouraging it to make use of them is one of the fun challenges the bird owner faces. The human's creativity needs to match the bird's and this is often harder than it sounds (see Toys, page 137).

Much of the stress in a parrot's life can come from feelings of being isolated from the flock. In the wild, parrots continually connect vocally with each other. These vocalizations are a source of security and entertainment. If humans, at least occasionally, respond to a bird's calls, then the bird will feel much more content. Playing vocal games back and forth by either singing or whistling and matching each others' notes can combat boredom. Repeating words by labeling actions and objects can lend predictability to the parrot's life. Often, the bird will learn the words associated with the objects or actions and be able to indicate

appreciate, which means more toward the UV. The manufacturer should provide this information.

Keeping a bird under lighting with a limited visual spectrum limits the colors the bird can see. This might be similar to a human trying to live under only "black light." While we could learn to function, some of us would be extremely stressed by the situation. Some individuals might seem fine, although they haven't experienced the light of day in decades. Others might experience amazing health improvements when provided full-spectrum lighting. Many grey parrots have been observed to regrow self-damaged feathers after the addition of this one additional environmental element.

## Sleep

Adequate, continuous, nighttime sleep is a very effective stress desires or needs, thereby increasing the bird's control over its life.

Sitting alone all day can be boring. No matter how many toys are in the cage or what radio station you leave playing, these are still very social animals. Parrots are very flexible in that they will welcome almost any creature as part of the flock. A cat or dog or canary or even a fish tank where the bird can see it can reduce boredom. Radio or television stations can be helpful also, but in trying to reduce boredom, it's best not to play the same radio station every day.

Changing anything can make the feather-mutilating problem worse, even if boredom was part of the problem. Sometimes it's better to allow the bird to increase its feather picking while it is adjusting to situations that will provide happiness in the future. At this time a collar to provide a physical barrier against picking can help a bird to adjust to a better situation while changing feather damaging habits for more appropriate habits.

## Toys, Enemies, and Environmental Enrichment

While the role of toys might seem frivolous to some humans, they provide companion birds with opportunities for decision making, manipulating parts, chewing, snuggling, talking, masturbating, and dominating. Multiple interesting toys with movable parts, chewable parts, and sound-producing parts will help to keep the bird occupied in ways other

### Shredable Fabric

A bird may be willing to chew on pure cotton fabric instead of feathers. Special care must be taken to ensure that the threads peeling off the raw edge of the fabric are not so long that they can wrap around little toes, restricting circulation and causing the loss of the toe. Woven goods about the weight of quilt or bandanna handkerchief fabric can be cut into strips along the bias, and no threads will peel off the edge. If the fabric is cut with the grain of the fabric, then the fabric can be clipped along the edge every inch (2.5 cm) so that the fibers peeling off the edge are only about an inch long. Tie these fabric "streamers" on toys, perches, or cage bars in places where the bird spends time. Some birds that shred filaments off feathers can be convinced to shred these short threads from the fabric. Paper pompoms and paper woven into cage bars or hung from treat holders can serve a similar function.

than grooming, overgrooming, chewing, snapping, or pulling feathers.

The development of a surrogate enemy toy is especially important, for that toy represents a flock member of lower status, and beating up the toy represents the maintenance of position in the pecking order to this highly status-conscious animal. An African grey parrot that does not have a surrogate enemy toy or a surrogate enemy among household members may be suffering from developmental failure that can lead to feather chewing.

A companion parrot that is not motivated to chew things other than feathers must be inspired to turn that beak to other elements of the environment. New, unpainted baskets, grapevine wreaths from the hobby store, clean, new little brooms, cardboard, paper, or fabric elements may be introduced to stimulate destructive chewing of external elements rather than feathers. Little plastic whisk brooms can be run through the dishwasher and raw-edge fabric must be specially prepared.

### Change

Changes in the environment can precipitate bouts of feather mutilation in a poorly socialized bird. Prepare the bird to accept and understand change early, as described in the section on page 23. Change of residence, moving the cage, rearranging the furniture, remodeling, redecorating, seasonal changes in decorations or in what goes on outside can cause insecurity or even panic.

• When moving or changing residences, try to keep as many things the same as possible. This is not a good time to replace cage or toys. Try to keep the bird out of the middle of the chaos; try to find someone who will board the bird and cage while things are getting settled. Take the bird on a visit to the new house before it is going to spend the night there.

• When rearranging furniture, remove the bird from the room while moving things around.

• Keep holiday decorations modest around the bird. Put blinking lights and mechanical moving things in a different room or away from where the bird is forced to pay constant attention to them.

• When introducing a parrot to a new cage, try to do it slowly. Although you consider the new cage an improvement, the bird might not. Remember that the cage is a major source of security to the bird and that changing it can really rattle the bird's self-confidence. If there is a significant negative reaction to a new cage, consider that replacing it might not be a good idea.

### Coordination and Confidence

**Coordination:** Good emotional health starts with confidence, and confidence in parrots develops first with physical coordination. Like all infants, baby parrots are occasionally clumsy. A baby bird with an inappropriate wing feather trim, too closely trimmed toenails, and inappropriate perches may be *very* clumsy. This is especially true of heavy-bodied birds such as baby African greys. In the wild, where a fallen baby parrot would be somebody's dinner, baby greys develop extremely sharp toenails as a survival mechanism. In the companion environment, sharp toenails can lead to anxiety by irritating the tender skin of the handler. Failure to allow those sharp toenails, however, combined with the use of smooth, hard perches can contribute to frequent falls resulting in damaged or broken feathers. This can, in turn, lead to the development of feather shredding. Add a little unintentional reinforcement or a little bad luck, and we can easily see the development of a behavioral feather chewing pattern.

**Confidence:** As previously discussed, confidence can also be enhanced by manipulating height. In some cases that means raising the height of the bird. However, some grey parrots dive down when frightened and may appear calmer and less threatened when they are housed low, possibly behind a plant or other obstacle designed to improve the bird's sense of safety.

Expect the bird's behavior to change as a result of height manipulations. Especially when treating feather picking related to fearfulness we can expect to see a little aggression appear. While this is not behavior we want to keep, it's a good transitional behavior because it shows that the bird is confident enough to defend its territory. A more confident bird is less likely to damage feathers. We can cure the developing aggression later, but unless we see the bird express a little territorial behavior, we can assume that this is a part of behavioral development this bird has not yet experienced, and this might be part of where the feather damage is coming from.

Some cautious, phobic, or merely shy birds benefit from having places

*Slippery perches and overgroomed nails can cause a grey to lose confidence and begin picking feathers.*

to hide. Often this is provided by covering a part of the top of the cage in a manner that allows the bird to go sit out of sight. Some birds actually need a hide box or a brightly colored fabric tent. Some birds are motivated to sexual behaviors by these "nest sites," which may have to be removed later.

## Grooming Wings and Nails

Inappropriate wing and nail grooming can contribute to self-inflicted feather damage, just as corrective grooming can assist in recovery. One source of independence for a bird is the ability to move around on its own. The bird's nails should not be so short as to prevent climbing and hanging. Nails that are too long can be just as harmful, since they might get caught in fabric or in cage parts, causing stress as the bird moves around. Sometimes merely correcting the clipping of the nails can precipitate a recovery from feather chewing.

Wings should be trimmed to allow the bird to safely flutter down without fear of an uncontrolled landing. A ragged or too-short wing feather trim can contribute to falls and to preening disorders. However, sometimes a ragged trim can be corrected with very sharp scissors. Many birds recover from an incident of self-inflicted feather damage when wing feathers are allowed to grow out completely, then trimmed only slightly after the bird learns to fly. These birds should also not be allowed outside uncontained.

The tip of the beak is also used in climbing and should be long and sharp enough to aid in both climbing and hanging. A bird that cannot climb around on the cage or play area without a fear of falling will often feel insecure due to the lack of control over its environment.

## Relationships

A well-adjusted African grey will form different types of relationships with different "flock members." This often includes forming a matelike bond with a favorite person. There may be a time when the bird seeks to solidify its relationship with this one person to the exclusion of other relationships. Many people will emotionally push the bird away in an attempt to keep the bird from "over-bonding." Rather than pulling away, the person should be guiding the bird to learn how to entertain itself and to learn security and self-confidence. Often, the bird will start forming better relationships with other people when it gets a good one going with the favorite person. If this person sets up predictable routines and patterns around which other things can be varied, the bird will be encouraged to be more curious and accepting of change. Paying less attention to the bird during its needy times can cause anxiety and insecurity that sometimes leads to feather destruction.

Changes in the perceived flock can be very upsetting to parrots and also be hard for the owners to control. Introducing new family members—human or animal—can lead to a jealous reaction often based in insecurity. To combat this insecurity, the favorite person can establish a routine before the new member arrives. The old flock member should always be tended to before new additions (see page 38). It doesn't hurt to praise the established bird after the newcomer gets its attention as well. This most loved person might avoid flaunting a relationship with a significant other in front of the bird. Anytime a parrot is faced with a situation it has no control over, it is going to be more prone to pick feathers.

When a flock member disappears, a sort of mourning period may ensue. Greys form long-term pair bonds. This does not mean that the bird will not form another bond when the original mate disappears, but the bird will miss the companion. This type of stress is commonly associated with self-inflicted feather damage. Maintaining a routine and spending time talking to the bird can sometimes help, even if the bird doesn't want to come out of the cage.

## Breeding Stress

Breeding stress is blamed in many cases of feather picking. Someone who owns a bird that damages its own feathers will often be told that the bird "just needs a mate." But there are birds in the wild without mates. They, most likely, do not destroy their own feathers. Many companion birds have found "mates" in their humans. It might be frustrating for the bird that the mate keeps wandering off without it, and this stress might contribute to feather picking. It is unlikely that hormones are the only factor. Giving a feather picker a mate will often result in the feather picker picking its mate as well. Breeding time is a stressful time for a bird and even those that are actively breeding might pull feathers at this time. The parrot owner must try to ensure that no other elements are adding to the bird's stress.

## Accidental Reinforcement

One of the most important but hardest things for a caregiver to do when a beloved bird starts destroying its own feathers is to *not* get excited. The first reaction is often to make a fuss. If the owner runs over and gives the bird attention or scolds it or gives it a treat every time a feather is damaged, then the grey will start pulling feathers to get its owner's attention. If possible, distract the bird *before* it starts picking at feathers. If this is not possible, try to remain neutral. If the owner simply *has* to do something, or if the episode is particularly bad, misting the bird with water while avoiding eye or vocal contact can distract the parrot. Many birds learn to pull feathers when their favorite people respond by begging them to stop.

*The human's reaction to feather picking can reinforce the behavior.*

## What to Do: The Feather Chewing Checklist

• Take the grey to an experienced avian veterinarian for a complete workup.

• Examine the environment for elements that might cause stress for the bird.

• Keep a journal of the bird's behavior so that it can be distracted to appropriate behaviors before a feather-chewing incident would begin.

• Manipulate the environment to enhance curiosity and confidence: Adjust height, cage, location of cage, hiding places, perches, and toys.

• Spend time assuring the bird that it will never be abandoned; establish a pattern of going away and coming back.

• Increase the bird's regular playtime with humans

• Increase access to rainfall (frequent drenching showers).

• Increase access to exercise, including daily flapping exercises, until the bird is slightly winded.

• Improve diet, eliminate salt, monitor fat.

• Provide full-spectrum lighting at least 8 hours daily.

• Ensure that the bird has a full 12 hours of sleep each night.

• Consider a better water source and change water more frequently.

• If you've seen little or no improvement by mid-summer, start over: Consult the veterinarian again, perhaps a different veterinarian. Each doctor might test for and look for different things and sometimes a slightly different medical perspective can find and eliminate physiological factors.

## Collars, Body Stockings, and Other Devices

Plastic collars called Elizabethan Collars are sometimes necessary to halt active, acute self-inflicted feather or skin damage. These devices, including the new tube types, are not to be considered cures for feather damage, but rather, they are temporary means of preventing the inappropriate habit. They are especially helpful when there is an obvious health-related issue such as a staph infection of the skin that is undeniably stimulating the bird to self-damage. These devices, combined with improved behavioral practice upon removal, are necessary and often quite beneficial.

In more behaviorally difficult cases, body stockings or "teaser" bandanna handkerchief devices designed to encourage the bird to chew on the device rather than to prevent chewing may also be of great value. This induces the bird to chew the fabric rather than on its own breast. These devices are sometimes needed long-term rather than simply as a transition. Because of the possibility that these fabric devices might get caught on something, they must be used only with careful supervision.

## Examination, Distraction, Reinforcement, and Judgmentalism

Examine the environment for newly added elements that might be stressful to the bird such as new art, light fixtures, carpeting, sound-producing clocks, other animals, or provocative humans. Try to protect the bird from loud construction or demolition noises as well as from other loud birds or animals. Consider the possibility that a human or other creatures in the home may be secretly provoking the bird.

Keep a journal to determine exactly when the bird is chewing feathers and exactly what is happening when the feather chewing occurs, including the favorite human's reaction. Once you know when the behavior is occurring, the bird can be distracted to other behaviors, such as showering or exercise before the feather chewing behavior begins.

Of course, at no time should a companion bird be reinforced for engaging in feather-damaging behavior. You must provide for, stimulate, and reinforce other appropriate behaviors. Too much attention paid to a feather-chewing bird can cause the continuation of the unwanted behaviors.

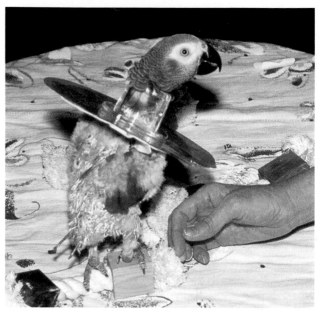

*Collars to prevent further damage may be required in extreme cases.*

Owners and caretakers should not be judged or criticized for owning a parrot with chewed feathers. Many caring humans have spent hundreds of dollars and thousands of hours working to help their birds recover from self-inflicted feather damage. Owning a feather-chewing parrot is not unlike having a teenager with a habit of nail biting or a fascination with tattoos or piercings. We can't withhold love from a beloved human or bird merely because we don't approve of that individual's personal grooming or ornamentation tastes.

[1] Colin Comb, D.V.M., lecture. 1998.

## Chapter Nine

# Recovering a Lost Grey Parrot

## The Grey Parrot That Flies Away

**B**ecause of their cautious natures, it's usually a little more difficult to recapture an African grey than other, more gregarious parrots. In the past, it was well known that a lost grey parrot probably wouldn't go to strangers. As more and more babies come up through well-socialized channels, however, we can expect this to change.

Prevention of the problem is preferred, but if the bird flies away, prompt action can mean more success. When an African grey flies away, work quickly. Try to keep the bird in sight. Have several spotters lined up so that if the bird flies, you'll see where it goes, and if it decides to go to someone, someone will be there. A hand-fed New World parrot will often go to almost any human by dark the first or second evening it is out. Many African parrots are so shy that they often will stay outside, terrified, hungry, and alone in the dark, rather than go to a stranger. This can work to their advantage if they wait to go to just the right person, and if they remain still and quiet, as is their nature, to avoid attracting predators.

By the second or third day, a lost hand-fed African grey should be very hungry, very thirsty, and very ready to find a friendly human. While this can ensure the bird's survival, there is no guarantee that this means the bird will be returned. Humans who find a bird are sometimes tempted to keep it. Rescuers might be judgmental about an owner who doesn't trim a bird's wing feathers. Depending upon the owner's intentions and practices, this might be a justifiable criticism. It is, therefore, important for the owner to immediately report a missing bird to police and animal control and to offer a reward for the bird's return. This demonstrates the owner's honorable intentions and dedication toward the bird. It establishes that the bird is lost property to be legally claimed.

## When You Don't Know Where the Bird Is

When you don't know where the bird is, the recapture project becomes first a public relations job:

**1.** You must advertise that the bird has been lost, offering a reward for its return. Call local humane societies, animal control authorities, local bird dealers, avian veterinarians, grommets, and recapture services. Place ads in the local newspapers, on church and grocery store bulletin boards.

**2.** Walk around the neighborhood and talk to people.

**3.** Occasionally blow an athletic whistle then listen for a response. Don't forget to look in all directions, as the bird will probably circle as soon as it figures out it is lost.

**4.** Be sure to report the loss to the police. If the bird is found and the people holding the bird won't relinquish it, the police may intervene. You must be able to prove ownership, possibly with a recorded band number, registered DNA configuration, microchipping, photos, or by records of unique physical or behavioral properties in the bird.

**5.** Make a flyer with a photo or a likeness of the bird. Prepare an 8½ × 11-inch (22 × 28 cm) white original so that it can be easily copied on to brightly colored paper. The flyer should contain a contact phone number, an alternate contact number, such as a pager, and the street corner or local landmark nearest to where the bird flew away. The flyer should mention small rewards available for information leading to the location of the bird and a more sizable reward for the bird's return. It's a good idea to minimize the value of the bird, possibly mentioning that the bird is not in good health, is noisy, or is of less-than-perfect disposition. You may mention identifying characteristics, such as a missing toe or banding on a particular leg. If the bird has a band, don't reveal the band number, so that the information can be used to differentiate between a person who really has your bird and an unscrupulous person who might be pretending to have your bird.

**6.** Talk with everyone you see, and make lots of flyers to post around the neighborhood and to hand to people. Use a different bright color each time the flyer is reprinted. If the recapture process lasts a while, the signs may have to be occasionally reposted after bad weather, and a new color will help people to understand that the search is still "fresh," and they should call if they see the bird. Don't forget to take your flyers down immediately upon recovering the bird. It's only polite, and in some places you may be fined if you do not take them down.

**7.** Don't give up. Keep looking. A bird doesn't usually just disappear.

On page 146 is a sample flyer for use in finding a lost companion African grey.

**Note:** It's a good idea to offer a substantial reward for the bird's return; in the case of a grey parrot, that might be $100 to $1,000. It's also good to advertise small rewards for any information about the bird's whereabouts.

# LOST PET BIRD

Virgil, an **AFRICAN GREY PARROT**

Lost on September 7, 1999
near Sheridan & Yale
in Lakewood, CO

A shy bird that probably won't go
to strangers, Virgil's feathers are
chewed revealing down on the breast

Virgil requires maintenance medication

*Substantial Reward for the bird's return*

*Small Rewards for any information leading to his return*

Call Mattie Sue at 333-555-1234 if you see
**A LARGE GRAY BIRD WITH A RED TAIL**

## Marty's Choice

Marty was vital, active, and wheelchair-bound. He was the long-time owner of an African grey parrot. One summer morning, as he emerged from the shower, Marty discovered that his wife had left the back door wide open when she went to work. On that particular morning, Marty had taken Ben, the grey parrot, into the shower with him. Turning the corner to the kitchen with Ben perched on his lap, they both saw the open back door, and at that exact moment,

the door behind them blew closed with a loud "Bang!"

Startled, Ben, who was scheduled for a wing trim that very day, flew out the back door. Marty, wet, dripping, and dressed only in a towel draped over his lap, followed out onto the patio in his rolling chair. There was Ben, perched in the fork of a young crabapple tree beside the picnic table. He was only inches out of reach, clicking and pinpointing his eyes, obviously enjoying his sunny freedom.

Marty took no time making his decision. Hoping that his neighbors weren't watching, he chose his bird over modesty. Pulling himself almost upright, Marty flipped the towel over his errant grey friend, pulled him from the fork of the tree, and wheeled, naked, back to the house with an angry grey parrot wrapped in the towel.

Ben would be on time for his wing-trimming appointment, and Marty would be avoiding his neighbors for a few days!

Remember, not everyone who finds a lost companion parrot is honest. It's not uncommon for a less-than-scrupulous stranger holding a lost African grey for ransom to have an exaggerated idea of the bird's actual material value. I like to mention on the flyer that the bird is somehow imperfect, and therefore, not especially valuable. With an older bird I might say

that the bird is known to attack or that it has daily medical needs.

## When You Know Where the Bird Is

If you know where the bird is, and it is in a high, inaccessible place, you can sometimes lure it down with a like bird, food, or jealousy. Sometimes the presence of the person the

*The food dish is lowered on a movable shelf until the bird must enter the cage to get it, and a human waiting out of sight pulls the door closed with a string.*

African grey parrot hates most will bring the bird down sooner than the presence of the most-beloved person. Especially, if the favorite person is expressing affection to the most hated rival, a African grey parrot will come down more quickly because of jealousy than with hunger.

If you have to climb a tree or other structure to get close enough to reach the bird, be sure to take a pillowcase with you. It's hard enough to hold onto an angry, full-flighted African grey, much less climb with one. Just tie the pillowcase in a knot to contain the bird and drop it carefully to a helper on the ground. If you must climb, be careful when using metal ladders around power lines. Electrocution is the most common cause of death or serious injury in a pet bird recapture accident. The safest possible climbing accessory is a cherry picker, a large piece of equipment that comes with a professional operator. In the

case of a grey parrot recapture, the bird will usually go only to a familiar person, so that is the person who must go up the tree or ladder or cherry picker to retrieve the bird.

Avoid the use of water hoses. Not only do hoses have an extremely short range, and it's often difficult to get close enough to the bird even to get it wet, but grey parrots can be excellent fliers, even when wet. It's highly unlikely that a good-flying African grey can be prevented from flying with water from a garden hose, and the strong pressure of water from a firefighter's hose could kill the bird.

On the other hand, those huge "Supersoaker" water guns can shoot a stream of water up to 50 feet (15 m). The bird can sometimes be herded to lower and lower places with the water gun, but this is very tricky and not recommended for African greys unless there is no other alternative, such as the case in which the bird is in a very inaccessible place. With this technique you run the risk of causing the bird to be even more wary and difficult to trap. It could also have long-term behavioral implications in a very reactionary bird.

Although capturing a free-flying hand-fed African grey might be as easy as walking up and saying "*Step-up!*" recapturing an experienced, human-wary feral African grey can seem a gargantuan task. The easiest way to capture a good-flying, human-shy bird is to first establish food dependency, then trap the bird. A trap can be easily made from a man-ufactured parrot cage lying on its back with a movable wire rack that can be placed at the top door to the cage. Place food first on a white dish on top of the cage. Each day, move the shelf lower into the cage. Within a few days, the bird will have to go into the cage to get the food, and you can pull the door closed, trapping the bird inside. It is also helpful to have a like species lure the bird within the trap-ping apparatus.

# When a Grey Parrot Is Stolen

Because hand-fed baby greys often relish cuddling, and because they are frequently accessible for handling by the public, babies are the most likely stolen African grey parrots. Greys appeal to both ama-teur and professional bird thieves because they are quiet, easy to snuggle into a coat lining or under a shirt, and very valuable for their rela-tively small size. This can be espe-cially tragic if the baby bird is being hand-fed or has other special needs.

Breeders and retailers must be watchful when unfamiliar groups come to look at babies. A typical theft scenario often involves one person, sometimes a child, making a scene or requiring assistance at a location away from where babies are kept, while an accomplice puts the baby bird inside a garment. Baby grey parrots should be accessible to unfamiliar individuals only with clean hands and with supervision.

## Chapter Ten
# Breeding Basics

In discussing breeding, you must be aware that there are so many pitfalls and risks to birds that information, references, equipment, and sound emergency backup must be in place well in advance of the arrival of offspring. Rick Jordan's *Parrot Incubation Procedures* (1990) and *Parrots: Hand-Feeding and Nursery Management* (with Howard Voren, 1992) provide invaluable instructions, even for those who plan to let the parents do most of that initial work. Even more germane to this text, Rick Jordan has coauthored a book on African parrots in aviculture with Jean Pattison, president of the African Parrot Society. I recommend that these books be read *before* a pair of grey parrots is set up to breed.

# Requirements for Successful Breeding

Aviculture is as much art as science. Specifics concerning cage dimensions and nest box styles are generalizations based on what has worked for other breeders.

## The Cage

The cage should be small enough to provide security, but large enough for the birds to move around freely. Minimum suggested dimensions are 4 feet long, 3 feet tall, and 2 feet wide (122 cm × 91 cm × 61 cm). Greys might breed in smaller cages, but many pairs would not be especially cooperative, and heartbreaking results such as injury to the mate, broken eggs, or injured chicks might appear.

## The Nest Box

L- or Z-shaped nest boxes typically work best for greys. Some greys chew wood during breeding season, so the boxes should be made of thick plywood and regularly inspected for extra holes. There should be an access door for checking eggs and removing babies.

The nest box should be outside the cage with the bird's access hole inside and the inspection door outside the cage. Most pairs will prefer a box that is located near the top of the cage. Some breeders give the pair a choice between two boxes. The view from the opening should be quiet and safe. The access hole should be about 3 inches (7.6 cm) across. If the birds want the hole larger, they will enlarge it by chewing the wood.

Pine shavings or paper-based litters are good nesting material. Corncob and crushed walnut shells can grow molds that are particularly harmful to the chicks. The oils in cedar shavings are potentially toxic. Paper from most paper shredders is too long and can become wrapped around the birds' legs or necks. Use nontoxic glue to adhere cork to the bottom of the nest box if the parents like to scoop the bedding out of the way. This will help prevent "spraddle leg."

# Obtaining a Pair

Of course, no breeding can be accomplished without a male and female bird. Ideally a breeder would pick sweet and well-adjusted birds to use as breeders as there is a good chance that these characteristics would be passed on to the babies. The problem is that everyone wants to keep the sweetest birds as pets.

There is also the option of choosing domestically bred birds for the parents, or imported birds. Imported birds are often nervous and a little more particular about their surroundings. Imported birds had been popularly used as breeders due to

*Shy, feather picking, or aggressive birds are poor choices for breeding.*

their low cost and prevalence; however, availability has steadily declined since imports into the United States were banned in 1992.

Domestically bred birds are usually more expensive unless they are, for some reason, no longer suitable as pets. Quite often, when a parrot has developed difficult behavior problems such as aggression, phobias, or feather plucking, there is a tendency to set these birds up for breeding. Unfortunately, these birds are exactly the ones that should not be bred. The future of greys in pet-oriented aviculture depends on producing birds whose temperament is suitable for life in captivity. Just as irresponsible reproduction of certain dog breeds has led to unpredictable or unacceptable temperaments, the same will happen with parrots if care is not taken to select premium individuals to pass on their genetic traits. Birds that are poor pets should not be bred to produce more birds that are poor pets.

# Gender and Bonding

While there are some differences in appearance between male and female greys, anyone pairing birds for breeding needs to have gender determined either by DNA or surgical sexing. Commercial kits are available for home use for DNA sexing. A drop of blood is collected from a toenail. This method is much easier on the bird than surgical sexing, although the parrot may require a day or two to recover from a sore toe.

In surgical sexing, the veterinarian puts the parrot under anesthesia and uses an endoscope to look inside it. By looking inside, the veterinarian will be able to get information about the bird's condition; however, there are risks involved with general anesthesia, including death.

Two birds of opposite gender do not automatically constitute a bonded pair; the birds must be willing to bond with each other. Love-at-first-sight pairs tend to be the most successful. If one of the birds can't stand the other, there is little chance of that bird changing its mind, and it would be best to find an alternate mate. Some hand-fed birds may be so human-oriented that they will be reluctant to form a bond with a parrot.

# Special Needs of Breeding Parrots

## Diet

Breeding parrots require a better diet than companion parrots. Any parrots that breed regularly, especially if they have two or three clutches yearly, will probably need additional Vitamin E and calcium. Any other dietary supplements should be evaluated and approved by an avian veterinarian.

## Lighting

Full-spectrum lighting enhances productivity. Lighting can be timed so that birds are provided with 12 hours of daylight and 12 hours of night, although variable lighting cycles can increase productivity.

## Grooming

Grey parrots often groom or naturally acquire very sharp toenails. Punctured eggs can result if this occurs during a breeding cycle. It's not a good idea to catch a laying or sitting grey parrot to groom her nails, so don't forget to carefully groom both parent's nails before the nest box goes up.

## Privacy

Grey are often very private breeders; copulation and related behaviors are seldom seen by humans. Many pairs appear to copulate only in the nest box and will not produce if they are disturbed too often.

# Stimulating Breeding Behaviors

While some breeders find they have no trouble at all stimulating breeding by merely feeding an exceptional diet such as Harrison's Bird Diet for Breeding Birds, some aviculturists report that they must use environmental manipulations to stimulate breeding behaviors.

• Add shortened "winter" days for about three weeks before breeding is desired.

• Add an artificial rainy season by increasing showers when breeding is desired.

• Change the diet, possibly providing an artificial harvest period where food is suddenly more abundant.

• Move the cage and/or nest box, or just take the birds for a ride in the car.

• Consider changing the direction the nest hole faces.

• Fill the nest box with shavings so that the birds will be stimulated by removing them.

# Eggs

The pair's food consumption will obviously increase, then decrease as laying begins. At this time, the birds should be given as much food as they will eat, especially calcium and protein-rich foods. The hen usually lays two to four eggs at two-day intervals.

As mentioned, the birds must be provided as much privacy as possible at this time. It may be difficult to socialize the birds to allow nest box inspection. Many greys sit tight and guard the eggs, with a chance of breaking them when disturbed. While some breeders advise not disturbing birds on eggs, we believe that good husbandry can save more eggs and more chicks if the birds have been conditioned to allow daily inspection of the nest box. Some pairs do not allow this. Again, the proper thing to do is know your birds and accommodate their needs.

A fertile egg can be detected after five to seven days, when blood vessels can be seen. Incubation typically lasts 24 to 26 days, although it can be delayed as long as four or five days.[1] Eggs need not be removed to be candled. Don't attempt to remove eggs while the parents are in the nest box; the parents could break the eggs and injure the keeper.

Once the eggs have hatched, parents need plenty of nutritional soft food. Their caloric intake should increase dramatically. Vegetables, cooked beans, and moistened whole grain bread are good foods that can be increased or added to the diet at this time. As chicks grow larger, the parents will require more calories.

# Care and Feeding of Chicks

If possible, the chicks should be left with their parents for the first ten days. When parents feed chicks, they incorporate digestive enzymes that allow the chicks to better absorb and utilize nutrients. Very young chicks have no ability to regulate body temperature and are very sensitive to temperature changes. They can become chilled during the time required for hand-feeding.

Baby parrots, especially greys, must be removed from the parents at an age young enough that they are not traumatized by the transition. Our experience has been that the chicks adapt easily to the new "parent" if removed from the nest by the time they are three weeks old. Leaving the babies in the nest longer is possible but some individual babies may not adapt easily.

## Temperature and Humidity

While there are guidelines for what temperature and humidity are best, adjustments should be made for the individual birds involved. A brooder with controls for temperature and humidity can save you a great deal of worry and guesswork. However, many babies have been raised without sophisticated equipment.

**Temperature:** For babies that are not yet covered with fuzzy gray down, the temperature should be between 90 and 95°F (32–35°C). If the babies are shivering or huddled together, the temperature should be raised slightly. If they are panting, the temperature should be reduced. Chicks should look comfortable. The more babies being kept together, the less added heat may be required. As the chicks develop, the temperature should gradually be reduced. Once the chicks are feathered, they should do quite well at 78°F (25°C).

**Humidity:** The humidity can be kept around 60 percent for most young chicks. It should be increased if the baby is showing signs of dehydration such as red skin. Red skin may also mean that the hand-feeding formula is too dry or that the baby has developed an infection. A consultation with an avian veterinarian may be necessary if the condition persists.

## Housing Needs

Until the chicks are ready to get up and start moving around on their own, they should be provided with a nest that allows enough room for all of the chicks, but not much extra. The bones in their legs are not hard at this point and may become deformed if the baby doesn't keep them tucked under. The bedding used should be something that the little parrots can get traction on. Cloth diapers work well as bedding. Washcloths and hand towels are not smooth enough, and the babies get their toenails caught in them.

Bedding should be changed several times daily. If there are several babies, a paper towel can be placed over the cloth and replaced between the times that the cloth is replaced.

Paper towels should not be used by themselves because they do not absorb as much as the diaper and get too cold when they are not completely dry. Especially in dry climates, moisture retained by the cloth can be beneficial by boosting humidity and keeping the babies from drying out.

As the babies get older, they can be moved to a container that allows them to move around. They will be too old for a brooder but may still need some added heat source. A 10-gallon (38 L) aquarium is easily converted as a brooder with shredded paper in the bottom and a heating pad under one end. Privacy is very important, as is the ability to peek out. Drape a towel over one end so that the babies can either hide in the security of the towel or come out and look around.

At this age the babies put all kinds of things in their mouths and can swallow them. The bedding should not be easily swallowed and not harmful if it is eaten. Wood shavings are not acceptable. Many organic litters can carry spores of fungus and bacteria that can become active when soiled by the baby birds. Paper from a paper shredder is useful as long as the strips are not more than one sheet long. Longer strips can get wrapped around the chick's legs or neck.

## Diet

There are many formulated diets to choose from, and they are not all created equal. By talking with local

*A paper cup, syringe, and pipette are easy-to-use hand-feeding tools.*

avian veterinarians and bird breeders, a grey breeder can find out what kinds of formulated diets are available in the area and which of those is best for the grey parrots. The labels of a few of them can then be compared (see section on nutrition, page 81) and a decision made as to which brand to try. The breeder should choose the formula before the chicks are hatched.

Instructions for use always come with the package of formula. Many breeders have ways of "doctoring" the formula, but this is not recommended as the results can be devastating. Changing formulas is also not recommended unless directed by a veterinarian.

## Hand-feeding

There are several hand-feeding tools to choose from and entire books have been written on this subject as well as on weaning the chicks. Hand-feeding is always best learned by example.

**Heating the formula:** Hand-feeding formula should be mixed according to instructions to a consistency that is easily delivered by the method chosen and is easily digested by the chick. The temperature should be brought to 104°F (40°C). Temperatures exceeding 43°F (6°C) could scald the crop, so using an accurate thermometer is essential. A hot water bath can be used to adjust the temperature. Heating formula in the microwave creates "hot spots" in the liquid. If fed to a baby bird, these hot portions can cause crop burn and death.

**Spoon-feeding:** One of the most preferred ways of administering the food is spoon-feeding. A spoon is used with the sides bent in a manner that resembles the parents' mandible, then filled with food with the end allowed to rest inside the baby's beak. The baby's feeding motion will allow food to fall from the spoon into the mouth, and the baby is allowed to take as much as it wants at a time. This method most closely resembles the way the chick would take food from the parent. It also requires the hand-feeder to spend more time with each individual youngster, a wonderful behavioral advantage.

**Feeding devices:** A syringe or pipette can be used to feed the little parrots. For this procedure it is helpful to understand some basic anatomy. The trachea opens at the base of the tongue. The esophagus is behind the trachea. In the throat the esophagus curves to the right and goes into the L-shaped crop.

The baby bird must hold its breath while the food passes over the trachea and into the crop. For the most part, this is a reflex action for the chick; however, keeping the food in the mouth for too long can result in the baby needing to breathe and aspirating some of the formula. Knowing that the esophagus curves over to the right side of the bird, many hand-feeders like to hold the syringe or pipette to the left side of the bird's mouth.

Sometimes, a hand-feeder will be nervous about the baby aspirating and as a result, will tube- or gavage-feed the babies. With this method a tube or feeding "needle" is inserted into the chick's crop. The food passes directly into the crop without touching the baby's mouth. As a hand-feeding technique, this method is less natural than other techniques discussed here. It is an invasive procedure and does not allow the little parrot to become accustomed to the taste and feeling of food in its mouth. This should not be considered a standard hand-feeding technique, but rather a solution for emergency situations.

**Nurturing time:** The amount of time spent with each baby is very important. The idea behind pulling the chicks from their nurturing parents is for them to associate that nurturing with human contact. Nurturing takes time; it is the purpose of hand-feeding. If there is too little time to cuddle each baby at feeding time, be sure to make time for cuddling later.

## Feeding Schedule

The crops of the chicks should be filled to bulging but not distended. When the crop has emptied, the baby should be fed again. The amount of time between feedings depends on the age of the chick and the amount of food the crop will hold as well as how thick the formula is and what kind of formula is used. The time between feedings should gradually increase as the bird steadily gains weight. Any sudden increase in the time it takes for the crop to empty would indicate that there is a problem.

## The Feeding Response

To elicit a regurgitation response from the parents, chicks grab the parent's beaks and pump in a rapid up-and-down motion. They also perform this behavior with each other and can be encouraged to perform it with the hand-feeder's fingers. This behavior is analogous to the sucking performed by human babies. As with young humans, the urge to solicit food is not always connected to the lack of or presence of food in the crop or stomach. While children can suck their thumbs, baby birds can not fill this need on their own. You must spend time allowing the babies to "suck" on fingers or feeding instruments so that the parrot can fill this need for itself. Allowing the little grey to fill this need is in no way teasing it; it can actually provide the chick with a feeling of security, similar to a child sucking its thumb.

## Weaning

The weaning process actually starts when the chick hatches and gets its first meal. Neglecting to consider this can make the weaning stage notoriously stressful and difficult for many young birds.

Parent greys and other parrots do not produce a special food for the baby birds as do some other bird species. From the very start, the baby is allowed to sample the different flavors and textures of the foods regularly eaten by the parents. These experiences are imprinted in the young bird and are what the weaning bird draws on when it begins feeding itself. A young bird that has reached the age of weaning, having experienced only the flavor and texture of hand-feeding formula, must overcome the effects of its sensory deprivation before it can learn to eat on its own.

While you cannot chew up food for baby parrots and mix it with digestive enzymes the way a parent bird does, there are ways you can provide this early sensory stimulation. At four or five weeks of age, the bird should have the appearance of being fully feathered from a top view, even though it may still be missing many of its body feathers. The chick will be producing enough of its own enzymes to be able to digest small amounts of crushed or minced vegetables. The vegetables should be wet and at the same temperature as the hand-feeding formula. Initially, you can put one or two pinches of food in the bird's

## Possible Causes for Failure of Crop to Empty (Crop Stasis)

• The formula is too thick.
• The chick is being subjected to suboptimal temperatures.
• The chick is dehydrated.
• The crop has a bacterial or fungal infection.
• The chick has a bacterial or viral infection.
• The chick was overfed at the last feeding.
• The chick is too hot.

*Young greys begin eating independently at different rates.*

mouth while you are eliciting the feeding response. You can then give the baby its formula as usual. The pinch of food will not digest as quickly as the formula but should be gone within 24 hours. The baby should be hand-fed as if the solid food were not there. If the solid food is not gone by the next day, the baby may not be old enough to handle the food yet. You should wait five to seven days before trying again. If the solid food is easily digested, the baby can be fed solid food once daily. The amount can be gradually increased as the baby becomes stronger and more able to digest the food.

Young greys are very visual as weaning nears. Showing the solid food to the baby as it is brought to its mouth will help the chick learn to associate the appearance of the food with eating it.

As soon as chicks are walking around and exploring their environment, they should be provided with low dishes of food. The babies will play with the food and drag it around their container. Gradually, they will begin eating more of it. Eventually, they will refuse the hand-feeding formula on a regular basis, although even a fully weaned bird may accept warm formula-like food on an occasional basis.

[1] Rick Jordan, *Parrot Incubation Procedures.* Silvio Mattacchione & Co., 1989.

# Glossary

Please note that the following definitions set forth the meanings of these words as they are used specifically in this text. They are not intended to be full and complete definitions.

**abundance weaning**: allowing a baby parrot to choose to eat solid food by offering excesses of solid food and as much hand-feeding formula as it desires.

**adaptive behaviors**: learned behaviors that increase the bird's chances of surviving by producing more offspring.

**adapted**: having adjusted to the environment in a positive manner

**Ailanthus**: "trees of heaven," so named for a Moluccan word meaning, "tree that grows up to the sky;" weed tree common in older urban cities in the United States. Soft, easy to grip branches well suited as African grey parrot perches.

**aggression**: hostile nipping, biting, or chasing.

**allofeeding**: mutual feeding or simulated mutual feeding. One of several behaviors related to breeding.

**allopreening**: mutual preening or simulated mutual preening, as in a human scratching a parrot's neck.

**altricial**: a bird that is helpless upon hatching and must be cared for by its parents.

**anthropomorphizing**: ascribing human attributes to a non-human thing.

**aviary birds**: birds that live in captivity, but in a bird-identified setting in which they do not interact on a regular basis with humans.

**baby days**: a young parrot's first, impressionable weeks in the new home, an idyllic period before the baby bird's instincts for independence, dominance, and exploration develop. *See also:* honeymoon period.

**band**: coded metal device placed around a bird's leg for identification purposes.

**barrier frustration**: a reaction to physical or visual barriers that can be used to stimulate confidence and vocalizations in companion parrots.

**beaking**: testing the feel of the beak on various substances, including skin by a baby parrot.

**behavioral environment**: behavioral conditions, especially redundant behaviors including habits, present in the bird and in individuals around the bird.

**bite**: use of the parrot's beak in a manner intended to cause damage or injury.

**bite zone**: area in front of the bird's beak in which the hand can easily be bitten but not easily stepped on (see page 108).

**blood feather**: unopened immature feather which is completely or partially covered by a bluish/white membrane indicating that the feather is currently supplied with blood.

**body language**: non-vocal communication involving posturing, displaying, or otherwise signaling an individual's feelings or intentions

**bonding**: the connection with another bird, a human, object, or location which a bird exhibits and defends.

**boredom**: stress caused in companion parrots by a lack of access to activities that they would be instinctually suited to experience including wild and self-rewarding companion pastimes.

**breeding-related behaviors**: behaviors with a source related to breeding habits in the wild such as chewing, emptying cavities, hiding in dark places, allopreening, allofeeding, masturbating, copulating, and aggression at the nest site (cage).

**cage bound**: so fixated on an unchanging environment that any change stimulates either aggression or fearfulness in a captive bird.

**cavity-breeding behaviors**: breeding-related behaviors of parrots including chewing, emptying cavities, fondness for small spaces, peeking out, and aggression at the nest site.

**chasing**: to drive away by pursuing.

**chewing**: breeding-related behavior involving destruction of wood or other shredable environmental elements.

**cloaca**: *also called* the vent. Part of birds' anatomy where waste materials are collected for excretion. Also opening where sperm or eggs are deposited.

**command**: an order or instruction given by a dominant individual.

**companion parrot**: a parrot that lives as a companion to humans.

**covert**: a layer of covering feathers as in the gray and green feathers covering the bird's down.

**creche**: a nursery group of juvenile parrots.

**crop stasis**: when food accumulates and will not pass through the crop, especially of a baby bird.

**cue**: a word or group of words established to stimulate certain behaviors.

**dander**: powder formed when discarded sheaths are removed from new feathers or powder that is contained in certain down feathers that is released when the bird preens.

**defensiveness**: occasional, mild, or infrequent territorial aggression.

**developmental period**: a period of rapid behavioral development wherein a parrot may demonstrate tendencies for dominance, independence, aggression, and panic. *See also:* terrible twos.

**diarrhea**: abnormal droppings that include undigested food in the feces or do not have three distinct parts. Diarrhea is accompanied by weight loss in the bird.

**dominance**: control, enforcing individual will over others.

**down**: the small fuzzy feathers next to the body that are normally covered by coverts.

**drama**: any activity that brings an exciting response, either positive or negative.

**eye contact**: the act of maintaining eye-to-eye gaze.

**family**: category ranking above genus.

**feather chewing**: self-inflicted feather damage involving damaging any part of the feather including the edges or the center shaft or rachis.

**feather cyst**: one or more feathers growing under the skin causing an uncomfortable abscess.

**feather mutilation**: self-induced damage to the feathers.

**feather picking**: used here to refer to any kind of self-inflicted feather damage including shredding, snapping, or plucking feathers from the follicles.

**feather plucking**: pulling feathers from the follicles.

**feather shredding**: self-inflicted damage to the edge of the barbs of the contour feathers, sometimes giving the feathers a hair-like appearance.

**feather snapping**: self-inflicted feather damage involving breaking off the center shaft or rachis.

**feather tracts**: symmetrical lines on bird's body where feathers grow in; especially visible on baby parrots.

**feces**: excreted solid waste, usually "worm like," which can be differentiated from urates and liquid urine.

**feral**: previously captive animals living in the wild.

**fight-or-flight response**: instinctual, automatic reaction to real or perceived danger.

**flashing**: a reaction in which the iris expands to the center, narrowing the pupils; this reaction denotes interest, especially interest necessary to develop speech. Also called pinpointing.

**fledge**: the act of learning to fly in order to leave the nest.

**flock/flock members**: as it applies to a companion bird, human companions sharing a home with a captive parrot.

**forage**: the search for and consumption of food.

**free feeding**: allowing access to food at all times.

**gavage**: a tube designed to deliver food or medicine directly into the crop; or the act of.

**genus**: a group of related species, usually sharing basic morphological and behavioral characteristics.

**good hand/bad hand**: a behavioral technique designed to distract a bird from biting (see page 55).

**grooming**: the process of having the companion parrot's wing feathers trimmed, nails cut or filed, and beak shaped, if necessary.

**habit**: redundant behavior that has become a fixed part of the bird's behavior.

**hand-fed**: a parrot that as a neonate was fed by humans rather than birds.

**handling techniques**: methods used by humans to stimulate and maintain successful tactile interactions with companion parrots.

**honeymoon period**: a young parrot's first, impressionable weeks in the new home, an idyllic period before the baby bird's instinct for dominance and exploration develop. *See also:* baby days.

**hookbill**: a parrot.

**human/mate**: the human companion chosen by the bird to fill the role of mate. The bird will perform courtship displays for this person and protect this person as it would a mate of the same species.

**imperfect**: a bird with an obvious physical defect resulting from congenital anomaly or injury.

**imprint**: to form a parent-like bond with the initial nurturer as a result of having been removed from the nest so early that the bird is confused as to what its parents look like. An imprinted bird will treat humans in the same manner it would treat another bird.

**independence**: improvising and enjoying self-rewarding behaviors.

**juvenile**: fully weaned, but immature grey parrots. Also, behaviors unrelated to nesting or breeding.

**keel bone**: the flat bone below the bird's crop that is attached perpendicular to the sternum.

**language**: vocal communication wherein multiple individuals use the same groups of sounds to convey the same meaning.

**maladaptive**: behaviors that decrease the bird's ability to function in its environment.

**Manzanita**: commercially available hardwood branches, which, in small sizes are suitable as perches for adult grey parrots with no gripping or perching problems.

**mandible**: the lower beak or horny protuberance with which the bird bites against the inside of the maxilla.

**mantling**: wing outstretching happiness behavior as described in falconry.

**masticate**: to chew, as in this case, with the beak.

**mate**: the individual to whom the parrot is primarily bonded. *See also:* human/mate.

**maxilla**: the upper beak; the notched protuberance that gives the hookbill its name.

**mimicking**: to copy modeled behavior, especially vocalizations.

**model**: a learning process by which one individual copies behavior from another individual.

**molt**: the cyclical shedding and replacing of feathers.

**neonate**: a baby parrot that cannot yet sustain itself by eating food independently. In the case of baby greys, these birds are usually being hand-fed.

**nest/nesting**: the act of constructing a structure for the purpose of reproduction.

**nest box**: a human-constructed box for bird nesting.

**nipping**: an accidental, unintentional, or nonaggressive pinch not intended to cause damage.

**normal**: the original animal that occurs wild. Not a color mutation (pied, lutino, or albino).

**parrot**: a hookbill; a bird with a notched maxilla, a mallet-shaped tongue, and four toes (two facing front and two facing back).

**patterning**: stimulating an individual to repeat behaviors through the process of repeatedly drilling the behavior.

**pecking order**: the hierarchy of dominance within a group of birds or their companions.

**phobic**: irrational or unexplainable fear.

**pinch**: a behavior designed to get a human's attention where the bird takes that person's skin in its beak and squeezes hard enough to cause pain, but not hard enough to break the skin.

**pinpointing**: a reaction in which the iris expands to the center, narrowing the pupils; this reaction denotes interest, especially interest necessary to develop speech. *Also called* flashing.

**polymer fume fever**: the condition that can kill a bird that is exposed to fumes from Teflon heated to 500°F.

**predator gaze**: to stare with both eyes straight-on in the manner of a predator with eyes on the front of its face.

**proen**: to groom the feathers, as with "combing" and "zipping" them with the beak.

**prompt**: a cue, here used for the physical cue to cause the bird to step-up.

**psittacine**: any parrot.

*Psittacus*: a genus of African grey parrots.

**quarantine**: enforced isolation for the prevention of disease transmission.

**reactive**: to quickly revert to instinctual reactions such as aggression or fear.

**recapture**: to apprehend or recover possession of a parrot that has flown away.

**regurgitate**: voluntary or involuntary production of partially digested food from the crop. *See also:* allofeeding.

**reinforce**: process of rewarding a behavior that we wish to become habitual.

**reprimand**: punishment; action intended to discourage a behavior.

**rescue**: fortuitous removal from frightening circumstances.

**rival**: a competitor, one who competes for reinforcement or reward.

**roaming**: unsupervised explorations away from approved cage or play areas.

**roost**: the place where a bird usually sleeps.

**scissor beak**: condition where the mandible overgrows the edge of the maxilla on one side.

**self-mutilation**: self-induced damage to the skin.

**self-rewarding behavior**: an activity that is enacted solely for the pleasure of doing it.

**sentinel/sentincl behavior**: a bird repeatedly or continually engaging in watchful and signaling behaviors intended to warn the flock of danger.

**sexual behavior**: self-rewarding breeding-related behavior.

**sexual maturity**: the period during which breeding-related behaviors become prominent in the bird's overall behavior.

**signaling**: anything—vocalization, tapping, or other body language—that warns, alerts, or telegraphs an intention or apparent impending behavior. A vocalization that falls short of true language.

**species:** subgenus; related groups of individuals that share common biological characteristics.

**spraddle leg:** a deformity that prevents normal use of any of the joints of the leg, usually causing the leg to bend outward.

**status:** positioning related to dominance within the pecking order.

**step-up:** practice of giving the step-up command with the expectation that the bird will perform the behavior.

**sternum:** the breastbone from which the keel bone protrudes.

**stress:** any stimulus, especially fear or pain, that inhibits normal psychological, physical, or behavioral balance.

**submission:** allowing another creature to demonstrate dominant status.

**subspecies:** a subdivision of species, especially by color or geographical characteristics.

**substratum:** material placed in the bottom of the bird's cage or play area to contain mess and droppings; plural, substrata.

**Sumac:** a small, sparsely branching weed tree found in pastures and adjoining land throughout most of the United States. Sumac is not poisonous, but rather is a common food source for many native species of birds. It is a little too soft to be good perches for African greys except as a transitional treatment for failure to chew.

**teaser:** a skin or feather-protection device designed to attract chewing behaviors to itself rather than preventing access to feathers.

**terrible twos:** a behavioral period wherein the bird's instincts for dominance, independence, and aggression are first manifest. *See also:* developmental period.

**"the thunderbolt":** a parrot's tendency to be smitten by love at first sight.

**tools:** an implement that is manipulated to accomplish a particular function.

**toxin:** any substance that causes illness or death through exposure to it.

**toy:** any tool for producing self-rewarding behavior.

**trap:** a device used to recapture a free-flying bird.

**urates:** nitrogenous wastes; the solid "white" part of a bird's excrement.

**urine:** clear, colorless liquid part of the bird's excrement.

**vent:** cloaca.

**vocabulary:** words or elements comprising a language.

**weaned:** capable of eating a variety of foods independent of help or supervision.

**window of opportunity:** a finite period during which something can be accomplished, a period of time during which behavior can be changed.

**wobble distraction:** a distraction performed during step-up practice (see page 49).

# Useful Addresses and Literature

## Organizations

The African Parrot Society
P.O. Box 204
Clarinda, IA 51632-2731

American Federation of Aviculture
P.O. Box 56218
Phoenix, AZ 85079

British Columbia Avicultural
   Society
11784 Ninth Avenue
North Delta, British Columbia
V4C 3H6
Canada

Canadian Parrot Association
32 Dronmore Court
Willowdale, Ontario
M2R 2H5
Canada

The Gabriel Foundation
P.O. Box 11477
Aspen, CO 81612

International Aviculturists Society
P.O. Box 2232
LaBelle, FL 33975

Oasis Parrot Sanctuary
P.O. Box 3104
Scottsdale, AZ 85271

The World Parrot Trust
P.O. Box 34114
Memphis, TN 38184

## Books

Athan, Mattie Sue. *Guide to a Well-Behaved Parrot.* 2d ed. Hauppauge, NY: Barron's Educational Series, Inc., 1999.

————. *Guide to Companion Parrot Behavior.* Hauppauge, NY: Barron's Educational Series, Inc., 1999.

Bergman, Petra. *Feeding Your Pet Bird.* Hauppauge, NY: Barron's Educational Series, Inc., 1993.

Forshaw, Joseph M. *Parrots of the World.* Neptune, NJ: T.F.H. Publications, Inc., 1977.

Gonzales, Fran. *African Greys.* Yorba Linda, CA: Neon Pet Publications, 1996.

Greeson, Linda. *Parrot Personalities.* Fruitland Park, FL: Greeson's Baby Parrots, 1993.

Harrison, Greg J., and Linda R. Harrison. *Clinical Avian Medicine and Surgery.* Philadelphia, PA: W. B. Saunders Co., 1986.

Jupiter, Tony, and Mike Parr. *Parrots: A Guide to Parrots of the World.* New Haven, CT: Yale University Press, 1998.

## Periodicals

*The AFA Watchbird*
2208 "A" Artesia Boulevard
Redondo Beach, CA 90278

*Bird Talk*
P.O. Box 6050
Mission Viejo, CA 92690

*Pet Bird Report*
2236 Mariner Square Drive #35
Alameda, CO 94501-6745

# Index